Contents

What's Inside This Book **4**

Using the Plays in This Book **6**

Things Could Always Be Worse 7

Frustrated by all the noise in his small house, Ruben asks the Rabbi to help him get some peace and quiet. Faithfully following the Rabbi's advice, Ruben finally discovers that things could always be worse.
* **Approximate running time: 15 minutes**
* **Roles: 14 characters, 1 narrator, 1 chorus, lots of chickens**

The Magic Pasta Pot 25

Luigi discovers that a magic pot makes Bella Nona's famous pasta perfecto. While Bella Nona is away, Luigi cooks pasta a-plenty, but he can't make the pot stop cooking!
* **Approximate running time: 15 minutes**
* **Roles: 8 characters, 1 pasta pot**

What Is an Elephant? 45

Six blind people each inspect just one part of an elephant and come up with a limited understanding of what an elephant is. Only when they start putting their thoughts together do they see the big picture.
* **Approximate running time: 11 minutes**
* **Roles: 7 characters, 1 chorus**

The King Who Would Not Laugh 61

A snooty king, who refuses to laugh or smile, comes up with a plan to reign forever. The king challenges his subjects to a contest he believes none of them can win.
* **Approximate running time: 15 minutes**
* **Roles: 13 characters, 1 storyteller (narrator)**

Dorothy in the Land of Blahs 79

One minute, Dorothy is playing an exciting new arcade game with her friends. The next minute, she's with a batch of Bobs in a dull, gray place called Blahs, trying to tame a wicked witch and then find her way back home.
* **Approximate running time: 17 minutes**
* **Roles: 8 characters, 2 narrators, 2 rainbows**

How to Make the Masks and Props **101**

Things Could Always Be Worse—Prop and Masks 102

The Magic Pasta Pot—Mask and Props 117

What Is an Elephant?—Elephant Prop Sections 129

The King Who Would Not Laugh—Masks and Props 145

Dorothy in the Land of Blahs—Masks and Props 163

What's Inside This Book

Students of every age love role-playing. *How to Do Plays from Favorite Tales* is designed to give students in grades 4 through 6, and beyond, role-playing and acting opportunities that also provide practice in oral fluency, creative expression, and cooperative learning and assist in building self-confidence. Performing plays promotes a variety of speaking and listening skills, as well as an understanding of literary elements. But best of all, performing plays is fun!

How to Do Plays from Favorite Tales is filled with easy dramatic activities that can be done right in the classroom. Five scripts and most of the materials needed to perform them are provided in this book. Each unit contains:

Teaching Guidelines

Suggestions for building background on the story line, characters, and script

A cast list, with ideas for adapting roles to suit your students' ability levels

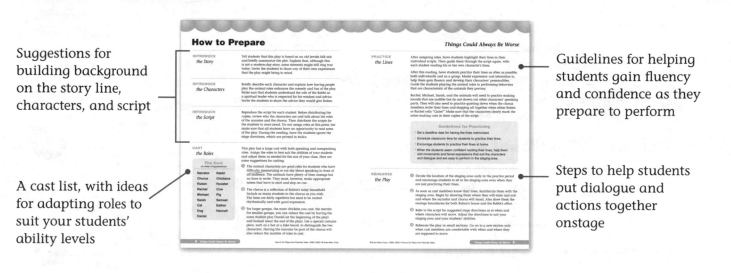

Guidelines for helping students gain fluency and confidence as they prepare to perform

Steps to help students put dialogue and actions together onstage

Quick and easy ways to turn classroom space into a staging area

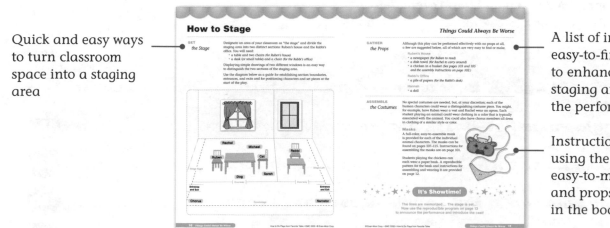

A list of inexpensive, easy-to-find props to enhance the staging area and the performance

Instructions for using the colorful, easy-to-make masks and props provided in the book

Reproducible Program

Students will love seeing their names publicized!

Production Activities

Reproducible patterns and detailed instructions make producing props easy and fun classroom activities.

Full-Color Masks and Props

These are real timesavers and meet all essential costume needs. Additional costuming is optional!

Script

Full-size pages with large type make lines easy to find and follow.

Simple stage directions make performing fun and easy.

Using the Plays in This Book

A play is more than just play. It is a means to purposeful learning. The five plays in *How to Do Plays from Favorite Tales* are not only fun to perform and easy to produce, but they also provide rich learning experiences.

Keep It Simple

- Take advantage of furniture and other items found in your classroom or in the school. Use them to set your staging area. Let students help you as crew members.

- Use pantomime instead of props. The few props that are suggested for some of the scripts serve mainly as prompts to help students remember and recite their lines, and all of the suggested props are easy to find or make.

- Set realistic goals. Encourage students to do their best, but don't expect perfection. If, for example, cast members have difficulty memorizing lines, allow them to read from their scripts. All of the plays are suitable for readers' theater activities as well as for classroom productions.

Make It Fun

- While cast members are rehearsing, engage any students who are not playing roles in "backstage" production activities, such as finding or making props, drawing and coloring the backdrop or mural for the staging area, or even helping the cast members practice their lines.

- Use theater vocabulary with the students to make the experience feel more authentic and special. Include basic words such as *set*, *script*, *characters*, and *performance*, as well as theater terms for stage positions. *(See the diagram at right.)*

- Keep enthusiasm and interest high. Allow students to have fun with the process and be sure that the time between introducing the play and giving the performance is kept to a minimum.

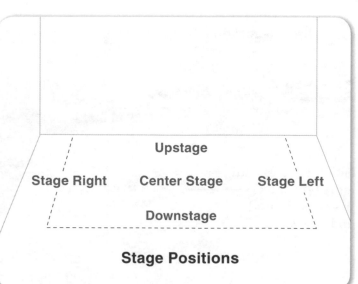

Upstage

Stage Right   Center Stage   Stage Left

Downstage

Stage Positions

Things Could Always Be Worse

Frustrated by all the noise in his small house, Ruben asks the Rabbi to help him get some peace and quiet. Faithfully following the Rabbi's advice, Ruben finally discovers that things could always be worse.

(Approximate running time: 15 minutes)

How to Prepare 8

How to Stage....................... 10

How to Make a Paper Beak......... 12

The Program 13

The Script 14

The Masks and Prop.......... 102–115

How to Prepare

INTRODUCE
the Story

Tell students that this play is based on an old Jewish folk tale and briefly summarize the plot. Explain that, although this is not a modern-day story, some elements might still ring true today. Invite the students to share any of their own experiences that the play might bring to mind.

INTRODUCE
the Characters

Briefly describe each character and explain how having people play the animal roles enhances the comedy and fun of the play. Make sure that students understand the role of the Rabbi as a spiritual leader who is respected for his wisdom and advice. Invite the students to share the advice they would give Ruben.

INTRODUCE
the Script

Reproduce the script for each student. Before distributing the copies, review who the characters are and talk about the roles of the narrator and the chorus. Then distribute the scripts for the students to read aloud. Do not assign roles at this point, but make sure that all students have an opportunity to read some of the play. During the reading, have the students ignore the stage directions, which are printed in italics.

CAST
the Roles

This play has a large cast with both speaking and nonspeaking roles. Assign the roles to best suit the abilities of your students and adjust them as needed for the size of your class. Here are some suggestions for casting:

The Cast
(in order of appearance)

Narrator	Rabbi
Chorus	Chickens
Ruben	Rooster
Rachel	Cow
Michael	Pig
Sarah	Samuel
Cat	Esther
Dog	Hannah
Daniel	

1. The animal characters are good roles for students who have difficulty memorizing or are shy about speaking in front of an audience. The animals have plenty of time onstage but no lines to recite. They must, however, make appropriate noises that have to start and stop on cue.

2. The chorus is a reflection of Ruben's noisy household. Include as many students in the chorus as you wish. The lines are fairly repetitive but need to be recited rhythmically and with good expression.

3. For larger groups, the more chickens you cast, the merrier. For smaller groups, you can reduce the cast by having the same student play Daniel (at the beginning of the play) and Samuel (near the end of the play). Use a special costume piece, such as a hat or a fake beard, to distinguish the two characters. Having the narrator be part of the chorus will also reduce the number of roles to cast.

PRACTICE
the Lines

After assigning roles, have students highlight their lines in their individual scripts. Then guide them through the script again, with each student reading his or her own character's lines.

After this reading, have students practice their lines as often as possible, both individually and as a group. Model expression and intonation to help them gain fluency and develop their characters' personalities. Guide the students playing the animal roles in performing behaviors that are characteristic of the animals they portray.

Rachel, Michael, Sarah, and the animals will need to practice making sounds that are audible but do not drown out other characters' speaking parts. They will also need to practice quieting down when the chorus members recite their lines and stopping all together when either Ruben or Rachel yells "Quiet!" Make sure that the characters clearly mark the noise-making cues in their copies of the script.

Guidelines for Practicing

- Set a deadline date for having the lines memorized.

- Schedule classroom time for students to practice their lines.

- Encourage students to practice their lines at home.

- When the students seem confident reciting their lines, help them add movements and facial expressions that suit the characters and dialogue and are easy to perform in the staging area.

REHEARSE
the Play

1. Decide the location of the staging area early in the practice period and encourage students to sit in the staging area even when they are just practicing their lines.

2. As soon as cast members know their lines, familiarize them with the staging area. Begin by showing them where they will enter and exit and where the narrator and chorus will stand. Also show them the onstage boundaries for both Ruben's house and the Rabbi's office.

3. Refer to the script for suggested stage directions as to when and where characters will move. Adjust the directions to suit your staging area and your students' abilities.

4. Rehearse the play in small sections. Go on to a new section only when cast members are comfortable with when and where they are supposed to move.

How to Stage

SET
the Stage

Designate an area of your classroom as "the stage" and divide the staging area into two distinct sections: Ruben's house and the Rabbi's office. You will need:
- a table and two chairs *(for Ruben's house)*
- a desk (or small table) and a chair *(for the Rabbi's office)*

Displaying simple drawings of two different windows is an easy way to distinguish the two sections of the staging area.

Use the diagram below as a guide for establishing section boundaries, entrances, and exits and for positioning characters and set pieces at the start of the play.

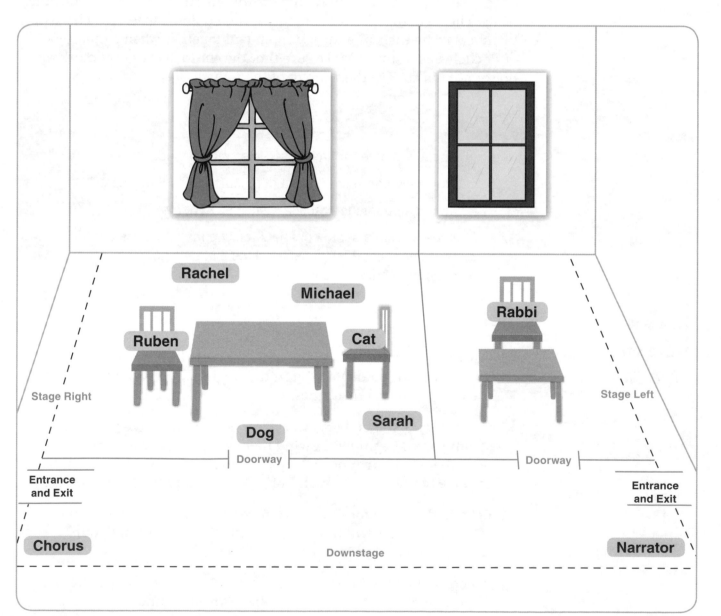

Rachel

Michael

Rabbi

Ruben

Cat

Stage Right

Stage Left

Sarah

Dog

Doorway

Doorway

Entrance and Exit

Entrance and Exit

Chorus

Downstage

Narrator

GATHER
the Props

Although this play can be performed effectively with no props at all, a few are suggested below, all of which are very easy to find or make.

Ruben's House
- a newspaper *(for Ruben to read)*
- a dish towel *(for Rachel to carry around)*
- a chicken in a basket *(See pages 103 and 105 and the assembly instructions on page 102.)*

Rabbi's Office
- a pile of papers *(for the Rabbi's desk)*

Hannah
- a doll

ASSEMBLE
the Costumes

No special costumes are needed, but, at your discretion, each of the human characters could wear a distinguishing costume piece. You might, for example, have Ruben wear a vest and Rachel wear an apron. Each student playing an animal could wear clothing in a color that is typically associated with the animal. You could also have chorus members all dress in clothing of a similar style or color.

Masks

A full-color, easy-to-assemble mask is provided for each of the individual animal characters. The masks can be found on pages 107–115. Instructions for assembling the masks are on page 101.

Students playing the chickens can each wear a paper beak. A reproducible pattern for the beak and instructions for assembling and wearing it are provided on page 12.

It's Showtime!

The lines are memorized … The stage is set …
Now use the reproducible program on page 13
to announce the performance and introduce the cast!

How to Make a Paper Beak

1. Reproduce the beak pattern below and give a copy to each student playing a chicken.

2. Have the students color their patterns and cut them out along the dashed lines.

3. Using the pattern as a template, trace around the beak shape on a piece of heavy construction paper and cut out the shape.

4. Glue the colored beak to the construction paper shape. *(For best results, use a glue stick or rubber cement.)*

5. Poke a small hole at each end of the pattern and apply hole reinforcements (on the back of the beak pattern only).

6. Thread heavy string or yarn through each hole and knot it securely in place.

7. Have the students wear the beak over the nose and tied at the back of the head.

Note: *If you prefer to laminate the beaks, skip steps 3 and 4 and do not apply hole reinforcements.*

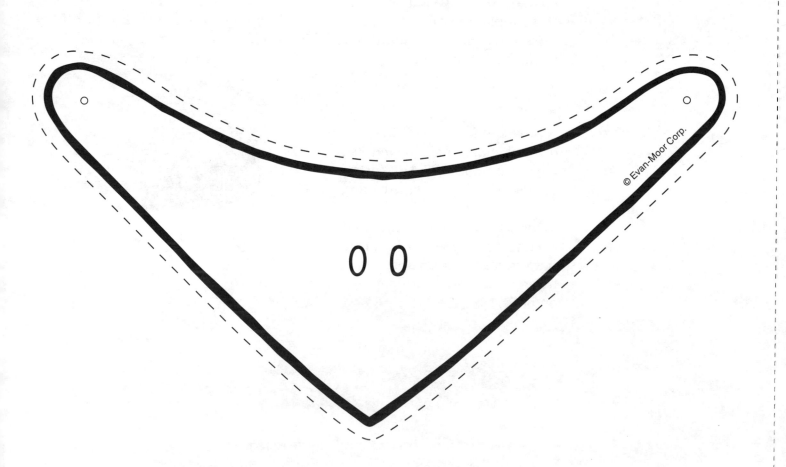

© Evan-Moor Corp.

Class: _____

presents the play

Things Could Always Be Worse

Starring

Narrator	_____	**Rooster**	_____
Ruben	_____	**Cow**	_____
Rachel	_____	**Pig**	_____
Michael	_____	**Samuel**	_____
Sarah	_____	**Esther**	_____
Cat	_____	**Hannah**	_____
Dog	_____	**Chorus**	_____
Daniel	_____		_____
Rabbi	_____		_____
Chickens	_____		_____
	_____		_____
	_____		_____

Things Could Always Be Worse

At the start of the play, **Narrator** and **Chorus** are downstage, far left and far right, respectively, and remain in these positions throughout the play. The **Rabbi** is working at his desk (stage left).

In the house (stage right), **Ruben** is sitting on the stage-right chair, holding a newspaper; **Rachel** is standing behind and slightly stage left of Ruben, singing off-key; **Michael** is upstage (behind the table), chasing **Sarah**, who is downstage center; a yowling **cat** is sitting on the chair at center stage; and a barking **dog** is on all fours on the floor in front of the table.

The noise in the house quiets down somewhat when the narrator or the chorus speaks.

Narrator:	Ruben and Rachel's house was very crowded and very lively.
Chorus:	*(hands over ears)* Shouting! Singing! Yowling! Barking! Such a racket! Such a fuss! Things could not be any worse.
Ruben:	Quiet! *(Noise stops. **Michael** and **Sarah** stop running.)* There is too much noise in this house! Please stop singing, Rachel. All this noise is driving me crazy!
Rachel:	Our house is small, Ruben. It will always be noisy in here.
Ruben:	*(stands)* Well, I can't stand it another minute! I need to get out for a while.
Rachel:	Don't you want your breakfast?
Ruben:	No, I'm too upset to eat.
Rachel:	Well then, don't be long, Ruben.

▶ **Ruben** leaves the house and walks stage left. **Characters in the house** freeze in position. **Daniel** enters stage left and meets Ruben.

Daniel:	Good morning, Ruben. How are you?

Ruben: *(sighs heavily)* I'm miserable, Daniel. My house is small, and the noise is terrible. My children shout. My wife sings off-key. The cat yowls and the dog barks. I never get a moment's peace! I don't know what to do.

Daniel: You poor man. Still, you should count your blessings, Ruben. A house is often a noisy place, but it is never a lonely one.

Ruben: *(walking stage right with Daniel)* Yet loneliness does bring peace and quiet, which is what I want right now. What can I do?

Daniel: Maybe the Rabbi can help you with your problem. He's a very wise man. Go talk to him.

Ruben: That's a good idea. I'll go see him right now.

Daniel: If it's any comfort to you, Ruben, things could not be any worse.

Ruben: Perhaps, my friend.

► *Ruben* and *Daniel* shake hands. *Daniel* exits stage right. *Ruben* walks stage left to the Rabbi's office.

Rabbi: *(looking up from his work)* Good morning, Ruben. It's good to see you. How are you and how is your wonderful family?

Ruben: Not good, Rabbi. My house is small, and the noise is terrible. My children shout. My wife sings off-key. The cat yowls and the dog barks. I am a good man, Rabbi. I do not deserve such a miserable life.

Rabbi: Hmm … Noise can be a problem, but I think I can help you. Tell me, Ruben, do you have any chickens?

Ruben: Chickens? Why, yes, I have chickens. But how will having chickens help me?

Rabbi: You must trust me, Ruben. I want you to bring all of your chickens into your house.

Ruben: Bring the chickens into my house? Rachel will be furious!

Rabbi: Do not doubt me, Ruben. You must do as I say.

Ruben: Yes, Rabbi, I will do as you say.

▶ *Ruben* exits stage right and reenters with two or more clucking chickens and the chicken-in-the-basket prop. He shoos the chickens into his house and sets the prop on the table. *Characters in the house* begin moving and speaking again when Ruben enters. *One chicken* jumps onto a chair, legs tucked under. *Other chickens* walk around or find a place to perch as they continue clucking.

Narrator: Ruben was very puzzled by the Rabbi's suggestion. But the Rabbi was a wise man, so Ruben did as the Rabbi said and shooed the chickens into his house.

Michael: Papa, what are you doing with our chickens?

Ruben: Well, Michael, I told the Rabbi that the noise around here makes me miserable, and he told me to bring all of our chickens into the house.

Sarah: What kind of advice is that? Where will the chickens lay their eggs? Do we need to bring in their nests, too? How long will they be staying in the house?

Ruben: You ask too many questions, Sarah.

Rachel: And you are too foolish, Ruben! The chickens will make a mess of our house!

Ruben: I must trust the Rabbi, Rachel. We shall have to make the best of it.

▶ *Ruben* shoos the chicken off the chair, picks up his newspaper, and sits. *Characters* resume their scripted noise-making activities, quieting down somewhat when the chorus speaks.

Chorus: *(hands over ears)*
Shouting! Singing! Yowling! Barking! Clucking! Clucking!
Such a racket! Such a fuss! Things could not be any worse.

Ruben: *(stands)* Quiet! *(Noise stops.)* The noise in here is awful!
These chickens have made the ruckus worse than before.
Perhaps I misunderstood the Rabbi's advice.

▶ *Ruben walks quickly to the Rabbi's office.* **Characters in the house** *freeze in position.*

Rabbi: Ruben! How are things with you and your family?

Ruben: Things are not good at all, Rabbi. My children shout.
My wife sings off-key. The cat yowls and the dog barks,
and NOW, the chickens go cluck, cluck, cluck at all hours.
I am a good man, Rabbi, and I do not deserve to be so
miserable. Please help me.

Rabbi: Tell me, Ruben, do you have a rooster?

Ruben: Yes, I have a grand rooster.

Rabbi: Good. Then bring the rooster into your house.

Ruben: Are you saying that a rooster will help with the noise?

Rabbi: Do not doubt me, Ruben. Just do as I say.

Ruben: Yes, Rabbi, I will do as you say.

▶ *Ruben exits stage right and reenters, coaxing a crowing rooster into the house.*
Rachel reacts with disbelief.

Narrator: Ruben coaxed the rooster into his house, where it strutted
and crowed among the chickens.

Sarah: Was the rooster lonely, Papa? Is that why you have brought
it into the house? *(Rooster crows; Michael imitates it.)*

Rachel: Ruben, are you out of your mind? I suppose you're going to tell me that the Rabbi said to bring the rooster into the house.

Ruben: In fact, the Rabbi did say to bring the rooster into the house, and we shall have to make the best of it!

► *Characters* resume their scripted noise-making activities, quieting down somewhat when the chorus speaks.

Chorus: *(hands over ears)*
Shouting! Singing! Yowling! Barking! Clucking! Crowing! Such a racket! Such a fuss! Things could not be any worse.

Ruben: Quiet! *(Noise stops.)* The rooster's squawking has made the noise even more terrible! Perhaps the Rabbi did not understand my problem. I must speak with him again.

► *Ruben* hurries to the Rabbi's office. *Characters in the house* freeze in position.

Ruben: Rabbi, you must listen to me. I have done everything you told me to do. But my children still shout. My wife still sings off-key. The cat still yowls. The dog still barks. The chickens are clucking at all hours, and NOW, the rooster crows, too. I am a good man, Rabbi, and I do not deserve to be so miserable. Do you understand my problem?

Rabbi: I assure you, Ruben, I do understand. Perhaps my advice was not complete. Do you have a cow and a pig?

Ruben: Yes, I have a fine cow and a plump pig. Surely you're not going to tell me to bring them into my house?

Rabbi: That is precisely what I'm going to tell you to do. You must move the cow and the pig into your house, Ruben. Do not question me. Just do as I say.

Ruben: *(audible sigh)* Very well, Rabbi. I will do as you say.

► *Ruben returns home, scratching his head with confusion. Then **Ruben** and **Michael** exit stage right and reenter, leading a mooing cow and an oinking pig into the house.*

Narrator: And so Ruben returned to his home, where he asked his son, Michael, to help him bring the family's cow and pig into the house.

Sarah: Papa, why must we have a muddy pig in the house?

Ruben: Because the Rabbi said we must.

Rachel: I don't understand the Rabbi's advice, Ruben. The problem is more than just noise now. The smell of all these animals is horrible.

Ruben: The Rabbi is a wise man, Rachel. We must trust his advice, and we shall have to make the best of it!

Rachel: Michael, get some straw and spread it around in here. We have to do something about the smell.

► *Michael exits stage right. **Characters** resume their scripted noise-making activities. **Michael** reenters stage right with imaginary straw and mimes spreading it around the house. The noise quiets down somewhat when the chorus speaks.*

Chorus: *(hands over ears)*
Shouting! Singing! Yowling! Barking!
Clucking! Crowing! Mooing! Oinking!
Such a racket! Such a fuss! Things could not be any worse.

Rachel: Quiet! *(Noise stops.)* I cannot stand all this noise!
Cluck, cluck, oink, oink, moo, moo, cock-a-doodle-doo!
It's all too much, Ruben! You must go speak with the Rabbi.
Perhaps you did not hear his instructions clearly.

► *Ruben runs to the Rabbi's office. **Characters in the house** freeze in position.*

Narrator: The Rabbi was not surprised to see Ruben again.

Rabbi: Ah, Ruben. I am happy to see you.
How are things today?

Ruben: Rabbi, Rabbi, I am miserable! I have done everything exactly
as you said, but my children still shout, my wife still sings
off-key, the cat yowls, the dog barks, the chickens cluck, the
rooster crows, and NOW, the cow moos and the pig oinks.
I am a good man, Rabbi, and I do not deserve to live this
way! I beg you to help me.

Rabbi: It is clear that your problem persists, Ruben. Tell me,
do you have any relatives that live nearby?

Ruben: Rachel's brother Samuel and his wife, Esther, live fairly close.

Rabbi: Do they have any children?

Ruben: Yes. They have a daughter.

Rabbi: Excellent! Invite them to stay at your house.

Ruben: But, Rabbi, there's no room!

Rabbi: Nonsense, Ruben, there is always room for family.
Now go and do as I say.

Ruben: Yes, Rabbi, I will do as you say.

▶ **Ruben** *returns to his house.* **Characters** *resume their scripted noise-making activities, with* **chickens**
sitting on both chairs. **Samuel, Esther,** *and* **Hannah** *enter stage right and go into Ruben's house.*

Narrator: And so Samuel and Esther and their daughter, Hannah,
came to stay with Ruben and Rachel. Rachel greeted her
brother's family warmly.

Rachel: *(moving downstage to greet Samuel's family)* I am so happy
to see you, Samuel! We haven't talked in a long time.
Esther, you look wonderful! And Hannah … my, how
you've grown! Come in! Sit down!

Esther:	Where will we sit? There are chickens on all the chairs.
Ruben:	Just shoo them off.
Samuel:	Why are all these animals inside your house, Rachel? You know that I'm allergic to fur and feathers.
Esther:	And look at this mess. There's straw everywhere—even on the stove! Is that a hen sitting in your bread basket, Rachel? Were these animals your idea, Ruben?
Ruben:	Actually, Esther, the Rabbi told me to bring the animals into the house.
Samuel:	Why would the Rabbi tell you such a thing?
Rachel:	Ruben went to see him to complain about too much noise.
Hannah:	I don't want to stay here, Mama. It stinks!
Esther:	Shh, Hannah. Don't be impolite.
Rachel:	Why don't I get you some bagels and cream cheese, Hannah. In fact, I'll get bagels and cream cheese for everyone!

► *Rachel sings as she pretends to prepare bagels and put them on the table.* **Hannah** *quickly helps herself and walks around with a bagel in her hand.* **Cow** *pretends to lick the cream cheese off Hannah's bagel.* **Michael, Sarah,** *and the* **animals** *continue to make their scripted noises, loud enough to be annoying, but quiet enough to hear other characters' lines.*

Hannah:	Papa! The cow is licking my bagel!
Samuel:	*(going after the cow)* Get away, cow! Go! Go!
Esther:	*(following Samuel and speaking in a very loud whisper)* No Rabbi would suggest bringing all these animals into the house, Samuel. I think Ruben made that up.

Samuel: *(shouting to Esther)* This racket is terrible, Esther! How will I sleep tonight?

Esther: *(shouting to Samuel)* What did you say? I can't hear you!

▶ *Pig grabs Hannah's doll.*

Hannah: *(chasing the pig)* Mama! The pig has my doll! Give me back my doll, you naughty pig!

Samuel: *(shouting)* I need some peace and quiet, Esther. I think we should go back to our house.

Esther: *(suddenly jumping back and screaming)* A mouse? Eeeek! Where? Where's the mouse? Get it, Samuel!

Samuel: *(shouting)* No, not a *mouse*, Esther. There's no mouse. I said *house*. Let's—go—*home*!

Esther: What? Why do you need a comb? I don't have a comb.

Hannah: *(squealing)* Grab the pig, Papa! Get my doll away from the pig!

Chorus: *(hands over ears)*
Shouting! Singing! Yowling! Barking! Clucking! Crowing!
Mooing! Oinking! Griping! Squealing!
Such a racket! Such a fuss! Things could not be any worse.

Narrator: There was no peace in Ruben's house. And just as Samuel reached out to grab the pig, Ruben let out a roar.

Ruben: QUIET! *(All noise and actions stop. No one moves except Ruben.)* This racket is unbearable! I must go to the Rabbi yet again! He got me into this misery, and he will have to get me out.

▶ *Ruben (extremely agitated) goes to the Rabbi.* **Characters in the house** *freeze in position.*

Rabbi: Ruben, what brings you here at this late hour?
Are things okay at your house?

Ruben: No, Rabbi! I am more miserable than ever before.
Now, three children are shouting. My wife continues to sing
off-key. *(starts making animals' sounds)* The cat ... *mmrrowww*s!
The dog ... *grrroof*s! The chickens ... *clu-cluck, clu-cluck*!
The rooster ... *er-er-er-er-er*s! The cow ... *moooooo*s! The
pig ... *oink-oink-oink*s! And NOW, my wife's family complains,
complains, complains!

Rabbi: *(escorting Ruben to the door)* Ah, Ruben, yes ... yes. The time has
come to send Samuel and his family home and to shoo your
animals back outside.

Ruben: *(scratching his head and mumbling with confusion)* Send Samuel?
Shoo the animals? But, Rabbi ...

Rabbi: Go now, Ruben. Do as I say.

Ruben: Yes, Rabbi. As always, I will do as you say.

► *Rabbi smiles and nods, watches Ruben leave, and then exits stage left. Ruben shuffles home,
muttering the Rabbi's instructions. Samuel's family waves goodbye and exits stage right.
Michael and Sarah help Ruben shoo the animals out of the house. Ruben passes the chicken
prop to one of the animals as they exit stage right. Rachel mimes housecleaning.*

Narrator: Ruben returned home and, once again, did as the Rabbi
had told him. Samuel and Esther were happy to leave.
Then Ruben and his children moved all the farm animals
out of the house while Rachel cleaned up the mess. When
the work was done, Ruben sat down and picked up his
newspaper. *(Ruben sits and picks up a newspaper.)*

Michael: All this work has made me hungry, Mama.
May I have a snack?

Sarah: *(squealing)* Me, too? I want the last piece of chocolate cake.

Michael: *(shouting)* No, I want the cake!

Rachel: Shh! Don't upset your father. I'll cut the piece of cake in half so you both can have some.

► *Michael* and *Sarah* argue. *Rachel* sings. *Cat* yowls. *Dog* barks.

Chorus: Shouting! Singing! Yowling! Barking!

Ruben: *(smiling)* My goodness, Rachel, isn't our home pleasant this evening? Our Rabbi is a very wise man.

Rachel: *(reacting with surprise)* But, Ruben, isn't the noise bothering you?

Ruben: Our house is small, Rachel. It will always be noisy in here. But things could ALWAYS be worse.

Narrator: Ruben and Rachel's house was very crowded and very lively, but NOW, Ruben liked it that way.

► *Narrator* exits stage left. *Chorus* exits stage right.
Michael noisily chases *Sarah* through the stage-right exit.
Ruben and *Rachel* follow, miming pleasant conversation.

The Magic Pasta Pot

Luigi discovers that a magic pot makes Bella Nona's famous pasta perfecto. While Bella Nona is away, Luigi cooks pasta a-plenty, but he can't make the pot stop cooking! **(Approximate running time: 15 minutes)**

How to Prepare 26

How to Stage........................... 28

How to Make the Pot and Pasta 30

The Program 31

The Script 32

The Mask and Props............. 117–127

How to Prepare

INTRODUCE
the Story

Tell students that this play is based on an Italian folk tale about an old woman who is well-known for making perfect pasta. Her secret is a magic pasta pot. One day, a villager discovers the secret. He uses the magic pot to make pasta for his friends, only to find that he can't make the pot stop cooking. Have students discuss the comic results this situation could cause.

INTRODUCE
the Characters

Introduce the old woman, Bella Nona. Explain that her name means "good grandmother." Then briefly describe the other characters in the story and how they depend on Bella Nona for help. Invite students to share any experiences they've had with older people who are good cooks or who do things to help others.

INTRODUCE
the Script

Reproduce the script for each student. Before distributing the copies, review who the characters are and talk briefly about how the roles of Linguini and The Pasta Pot add to the play's humor. Then distribute the scripts for the students to read aloud. Do not assign roles at this point, but make sure that all students have an opportunity to read some of the play. During the reading, have the students ignore the stage directions, which are printed in italics.

CAST
the Roles

The Cast
(in order of appearance)

Bella Nona

Linguini (a cat)

Gina

Maria

Carlo

Sergio

Luigi

The Pasta Pot

Carmela

Assign the roles to best suit the size of your class and the abilities of your students. Here are some suggestions for casting:

❶ All of the speaking roles, except Carmela, have a significant number of lines to learn, but the roles of Bella Nona and Luigi are by far the most challenging and are best suited to students with high levels of confidence and motivation.

❷ The part of the cat, Linguini, is entirely pantomimed. The student who plays this role should be a bit of a ham but know not to draw attention away from a speaker. The student must also be able to handle being onstage for the entire play.

❸ The role of The Pasta Pot could be assigned to a student who is hesitant to perform but would benefit from being part of the cast. He or she hides behind the table, displaying the spaghetti and tossing paper noodles as directed in the script.

❹ You can expand the cast by having more villagers join Gina, Maria, Carlo, Sergio, and Carmela. They will not have lines to recite, but they will have to pantomime speaking and reacting to the other characters.

PRACTICE
the Lines

After assigning the roles, have students highlight their lines in their individual scripts. Then guide them through the script again, with each student reading his or her own character's lines.

After this reading, have students practice their lines as often as possible, both individually and as a group. Model expression and intonation to help them gain fluency and develop their characters' personalities.

Assemble the pasta pot and make the paper noodles early in the practice period so the student controlling these props can perfect how and when to make pasta come out of the pot. Bella Nona should practice bursting the balloon prop (Carlo's wart) as often as possible, but could pantomime the action, with or without a balloon, until a few rehearsals before the performance.

Guidelines for Practicing

• Set a deadline date for having the lines memorized.

• Schedule classroom time for students to practice their lines.

• Encourage students to practice their lines at home.

• When the students seem confident reciting their lines, help them add movements and facial expressions that suit the characters and dialogue and are easy to perform in the staging area.

REHEARSE
the Play

❶ Decide the location of the staging area early in the practice period and encourage students to sit in the staging area even when they are just practicing their lines.

❷ As soon as cast members know their lines, familiarize them with the staging area. Begin by showing them where they will enter and exit and the positions of the characters, set pieces, and props that are onstage when the play starts.

❸ Refer to the script for suggested stage directions as to when and where characters will move. Adjust the directions to suit your staging area and your students' abilities.

❹ Rehearse the play in small sections. Go on to a new section only when cast members are comfortable with when and where they are supposed to move.

How to Stage

SET

the Stage

Designate an area of your classroom as "the stage." All of the action in the play takes place inside and in front of Bella Nona's house. You will need:

- a long table
- a tablecloth or blanket that is large enough to fully cover the table
- 2 chairs *(to indicate the doorway)*, with one chair facing upstage and the other facing downstage. The pasta pot prop should be visible through the doorway.

Displaying a simple drawing or mural of tall sunflowers is an easy way to transform part of the staging area into Bella Nona's garden.

Use the diagram below as a guide for establishing entrances and exits and for positioning characters, set pieces, and props at the start of the play.

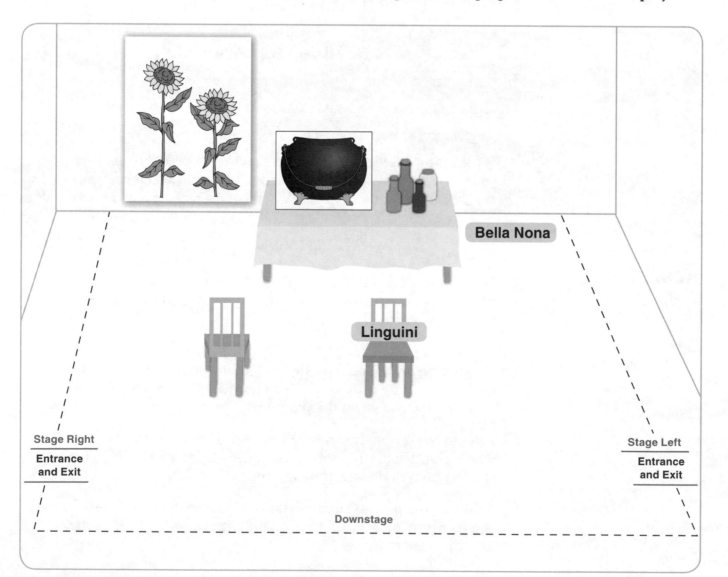

Bella Nona

Linguini

Stage Right
Entrance and Exit

Stage Left
Entrance and Exit

Downstage

GATHER
the Props

Using a few key props enhances the performance and helps characters recall their lines and movements. All of the props suggested below are easy to find or make and invite additional student participation.

- several plastic bottles *(various sizes)* filled with colored water
- the pasta pot and spaghetti, which are provided on pages 119–127. The instructions for how to assemble and use these props are on page 30.
- oodles of paper noodles *(See page 30.)*
- a small pink balloon with a short piece of string tied to it *(for the wart on Carlo's finger)*
- a colorful handkerchief or similar sized piece of cloth with a straight pin sticking through it
- a handprinted "Help Wanted" sign *(see right)*

Help Wanted

Gardening and
Housework
Pasta as Payment.
See Bella Nona

All props except the balloon should be preset in the staging area at the start of the play.

ASSEMBLE
the Costumes

Costumes can be as simple or elaborate as you wish, but no special costumes are needed. At your discretion, each character could wear a distinguishing costume piece, such as a shawl, scarf, necklace, bracelet, or hat. Allowing the students to suggest and find their own costume pieces is a good way to help them develop their characters.

Mask

The student playing Bella Nona's cat, Linguini, can wear the full-color mask found on page 117. The directions for assembling the mask are on page 101. You might also wish to have the student wear clothing in a color that matches or complements the mask.

It's Showtime!

The lines are memorized ... The stage is set ...
Now use the reproducible program on page 31
to announce the performance and introduce the cast!

How to Make the Pot and Pasta

The
Pasta Pot

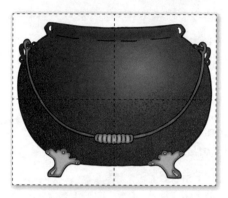

1. Cut out the four sections of the pasta pot. *(See pages 119–125.)* Laminate them, if possible, for added durability.

2. Fit the sections together to form the pot and glue them onto a piece of very stiff or corrugated cardboard. If the sections are laminated, use double-sided tape instead of glue.

3. Stand the assembled pot up against a metal bookend, or attach it to one side of a sturdy box, to hold it upright on the table in the staging area. Ideally, whatever is used to hold up the pot should not be visible to the audience.

The
Spaghetti

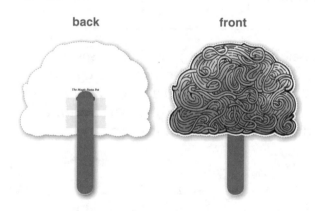

back   front

1. Cut out the spaghetti on page 127. Laminate it, if possible, for added durability.

2. Use glue or tape to attach a large craft stick to the back of the spaghetti. Tape 2 to 3 inches (5 to 8 cm) of the craft stick to the bottom of the spaghetti, leaving about a 4-inch (10-cm) handle for manipulating the prop.

The
Paper Noodles

1. Cut white paper into strips that are ½ inch (1.25 cm) wide and various lengths.

2. Wrap each strip around a pencil to make curly paper pasta noodles.

3. Make as much paper pasta as possible. The more pasta you have, the funnier the scene will appear to the audience.

4. Hide the paper pasta noodles behind the pasta pot or under the table so the student controlling the pasta pot will have easy access to them for tossing onto the stage.

Class: _____

presents the play

The **Magic Pasta Pot**

Starring

Bella Nona _____

Linguini _____

Gina _____

Maria _____

Carlo _____

Sergio _____

Luigi _____

Carmela _____

The Pasta Pot _____

The Magic Pasta Pot

At the start of the play, **Bella Nona** is in her house, working with bottles of potions (colored water) preset at one end of a long covered table. The pasta pot prop is at the opposite end of the table, and the student who will control the pasta is hiding under the table. **Linguini** is asleep on the stage-left (doorway) chair.

▶ *Gina and Maria enter stage right.*

Gina:	What's the matter, Maria? You're very quiet today.
Maria:	You won't believe the headache I've got, Gina. I can't eat. I can't sleep. I can't make it go away. What can I do about it?
Gina:	If I were you, I'd go see Bella Nona. She has potions that can cure anything.
Maria:	Bella Nona? Are you telling me that the woman known for her perfect pasta also makes perfect potions?
Gina:	That's what my mother tells me. She's worth a try, isn't she? *(teasing)* Maybe she'll cover your noggin with noodles. *(mimes draping noodles over Maria's head)*
Maria:	Very funny, Gina. But I think I will take your advice. Bella Nona lives right nearby. I'll stop in to see if she can help me.

▶ *Gina exits stage left. **Bella Nona** moves to the doorway as **Maria** approaches. **Linguini** wakes up and performs catlike actions that do not draw attention away from the main action of the scene.*

Bella Nona:	Good morning, Maria. Poor child, you look miserable. What's wrong?
Maria:	I have a terrible headache, Bella Nona. I've taken aspirin. I've rubbed my temples. I've put a cold pack on my eyes. Nothing will make this headache go away. Can you help me?

Bella Nona:	Come in, Maria. *(indicating stage-right chair)* Sit here and rest. I will mix a potion for you.

▶ *Maria enters the house and sits on the stage-right chair. Bella Nona mimes preparing a potion and takes it to Maria.*

Bella Nona:	Here you are, dear. Drink this. You should feel better soon.
Maria:	What's in it? Will it taste awful?
Bella Nona:	It's just a little of this and a little of that, and they're all things that are good for you. Drink up.

▶ *Maria skeptically drinks, then smiles.*

Maria:	Why, my headache is better already! You're wonderful, Bella Nona! Thank you! Your potion must be magic.
Bella Nona:	*(modestly)* Oh … no. It's not magic. When I was a little girl, my grandmother taught me how to use herbs and other plants to ease pain. I'm happy to help you, Maria. Now go and enjoy the day.

▶ *Maria waves goodbye to Bella Nona as she passes through the doorway of the house and walks stage left. Carlo enters stage left and meets Maria.*

Maria:	*Ciao (pronounced "chow")*, Carlo. *(noticing the balloon "wart" on Carlo's finger)* Eeeww! What in the world is that on your finger?
Carlo:	It's a wart, and it's driving me crazy. It grows bigger every day. I can't harvest my grapes because the wart keeps catching on the vines. Do you know anything about warts? Can you tell me how to get rid of it?
Maria:	I've never had a wart, Carlo, but I'll bet Bella Nona can help you. She told me that her grandmother taught her lots of cures.
Carlo:	Bella Nona? The pasta lady?

Maria: Yes. I just saw her, and she cured my headache just like that! *(snaps fingers)* I'll bet she can make your wart go away. You should stop at her house right now, before that thing gets any bigger … or uglier!

Carlo: I guess it can't hurt to stop in. Thanks, Maria!

▶ *Maria exits stage left.* **Carlo** *goes to Bella Nona's house.* **Bella Nona** *is at the doorway.*

Bella Nona: Carlo! I haven't seen you in a long time. Shouldn't you be in your vineyard, harvesting the grapes? *(glancing at the wart)* Oh my! That's the largest wart I've ever seen!

Carlo: It's also the most hideous! And it grows bigger every day, Bella Nona. I can't work in the fields because no glove is big enough to fit over it. Maria said that you can cure anything. Do you know how to get rid of warts?

Bella Nona: Of course I do. Come in and sit down. I just need to get some herbs and a special cloth my grandmother once gave me.

▶ **Bella Nona** *pretends to spread some herbs on a cloth that has a straight pin sticking through it.*

Bella Nona: *(approaching Carlo)* Now sit very still. We'll be done in a jiffy.

▶ **Bella Nona** *holds the cloth over Carlo's hand, punctures the balloon with the pin, and hides the broken balloon in the cloth as she removes it.* **Linguini** *reacts when the balloon pops.*

Carlo: Wow! The wart is gone! I can work again! Thank you, Bella Nona! I will bring you a bottle of my finest wine to repay you.

Bella Nona: I would like that very much. You have a good day, Carlo.

Carlo: I will. You have a good day, too, Bella Nona.

▶ **Bella Nona** *stands in the doorway waving goodbye to Carlo.* **Carlo** *exits stage right, smiling broadly, as* **Sergio** *enters stage left, looking downcast and shuffling along.*

Bella Nona:	My goodness, Sergio, you look as if the life has been squeezed out of you.
Sergio:	I am miserable, Bella Nona. My heart is broken.
Bella Nona:	A heart breaks only when it has loved and lost. Does your sadness have anything to do with Gina?
Sergio:	Yes, Gina has broken my heart. I am so in love with her, but she won't even speak to me. I have sent her flowers and written poems, but … it's no use. I should give up.
Bella Nona:	Nonsense. You are a wonderful boy, Sergio, and Gina is fortunate to have captured your heart. Wait here. I have something that might help Gina see you in a new way.

▶ *Bella Nona enters her house, quickly mixes up a potion, and brings it to Sergio.*

Sergio:	*(taking a whiff of the potion)* What is this? It smells like lavender and cinnamon.
Bella Nona:	Just take a swallow. Bella Nona knows what's good for you.
Sergio:	Okay. Here goes. *(drinks)* Hmm … how interesting. My heart doesn't feel so heavy anymore. In fact, I feel happy and confident! Thank you, Bella Nona.

▶ *Bella Nona and Linguini watch from the doorway as Sergio struts stage left and Gina enters stage left. They stop and look at each other, then Gina smiles at Sergio. Sergio turns and takes big steps toward the stage-right exit. Gina follows him, shouting.*

Gina:	Sergio! Stop! Wait for me! Wait … please … *(exits stage right)*
Bella Nona:	Ah, Linguini, love does strange things.

▶ *Linguini rubs head against Bella Nona's leg. Bella Nona stoops down to pat the cat's head.*

Bella Nona: Oof! Oh dear. There goes my back again.
I'm getting old, Linguini. My back aches when I try
to work in the garden. My eyes no longer see the dust
in the corners when I clean the house. I wish I could
hire someone to help me. But how can I? I can't afford
to pay a wage.

▶ *Linguini meows and points at the pasta pot.*

Bella Nona: What a good idea, Linguini! I can pay with pasta.
Who would not be happy to work for my perfect pasta?
Let's see then. I'll have to make a sign.

▶ *Bella Nona looks around for paper and a marker and pretends to write a sign (premade prop is under the table). She shows the sign to Linguini (who nods in approval) and then places it on the stage-left chair at the doorway. Going back inside the house, **Bella Nona** busies herself with her back to the doorway. **Luigi** enters stage left and stops at the sign. He faces the audience and reads the sign.*

Luigi: *(reading)* Help Wanted. *(addressing the audience)* I need work!
(reading) Gardening and Housework.
(to the audience) That kind of work is easy. Even I could do it!
(reading) Pasta as Payment. See Bella Nona.
(to the audience) Everyone knows Bella Nona makes the best
pasta in the village. For a little bit of work, I can eat her pasta
every day! *(calling through the doorway)* Bella Nona! Bella Nona!

Bella Nona: *(coming to the doorway)* Yes? How can I help you?

Luigi: I am Luigi, *(holds up the sign)* and I am here to help you.
I am very strong and very hungry. Do you have some
pasta for me?

Bella Nona: *(examining Luigi)* Hmm … If you want some pasta, you will have
to weed the garden, clean the house, and do any other work
I ask you to do.

Luigi: I will do whatever needs to be done. What do you have
for me to eat?

Bella Nona: You have to earn your food, Luigi. Go to the garden behind the house and pull the weeds. I will start boiling the pasta water, and I will call you when the pasta is ready.

► *Luigi hands Bella Nona the sign and turns to leave.* **Bella Nona** *and* **Linguini** *stand with their backs to the doorway, near the pasta pot but not blocking it from view.* **Luigi** *turns back and peeks through the doorway when he hears Bella Nona speak.*

Bella Nona: Bubble, bubble, pasta pot.
Make me noodles, nice and hot.
Pasta cooked 'til it's just right
Is perfect pasta, every bite.

(Spaghetti prop is slowly raised behind the pot and is held in place above the rim of the pot.)

That should be enough pasta for Luigi.

Please stop cooking, pasta pot.
I have noodles, nice and hot.
Your perfect pasta is the best.
Now it's time for you to rest.

► *Luigi dashes off to the garden and does not see* **Bella Nona** *press the fingertips of her right hand to her lips and throw a kiss to the pasta pot.* **Linguini** *mimics the kiss.*

Bella Nona: *(calling from the doorway)* Luigi! Come in now to eat some pasta.

Luigi: *(talking to himself as he walks to the doorway)* So Bella Nona has a magic pasta pot … What good fortune for me! *(enters the house)*

Bella Nona: Did you begin the weeding, Luigi?

Luigi: Yes, Bella Nona. Mmmm! Your pasta smells delicious. I have heard that you make perfect pasta—pasta perfecto!

Bella Nona: *(mimes giving Luigi a bowl and a fork)* Sit and eat now. I must take some medicine to my friend who is ill. When you have finished your pasta, wash your plate and all of the other dishes in the sink. But do not wash the pasta pot. Do not even touch the pasta pot. Do you hear me, Luigi? Do *not* touch the pasta pot!

Luigi:	I hear you, Bella Nona. I will wash the dishes, and I will *not* touch the pasta pot.
Bella Nona:	Good! Now eat your pasta before it gets cold.

▶ *Bella Nona grabs a bottle of potion and exits stage left.*
Gina, Sergio, and Carlo enter stage right. Maria and Carmela enter stage left.
The two groups meet at stage right and mime conversation.

Luigi:	*(to himself)* Ha! I have a magic pasta pot! I can make pasta for everyone! People will rave about me. I will be the most popular man in the village! *(pokes his head out the doorway)*
Sergio:	*(noticing Luigi and waving)* Luigi! How are you? Look, everyone. It's Luigi!
Luigi:	*(motioning to the group)* Come in, come in! I will make all the pasta you can eat!
Gina:	What are you talking about, Luigi? You've never cooked a good meal in your life.
Carmela:	What are you doing in Bella Nona's house, Luigi?
Luigi:	For your information, Carmela, I am Bella Nona's trusted servant and cook, and I am going to make you the finest pasta you've ever tasted! Now go get your plates and forks! *(goes back inside the house)*
Carmela:	I've never known Luigi to be good at anything, especially cooking.
Maria:	Who knows? Maybe Bella Nona taught him how to make her pasta perfecto.
Carlo:	Well, there's only one way to find out. I'm going to get a plate and a fork.
Carmela:	Wait, Carlo. I'll go with you.

Maria: Me too, Carlo.

▶ *Carlo, Carmela, and Maria exit stage right. Sergio and Gina shake their heads and exit stage left.*

Luigi: Now, what did Bella Nona say to make the pot work?

Bubble, bubble, pasta pot.
Make me noodles, nice and hot.
Pasta cooked 'til it's just right
Is perfect pasta, every piece.

(Pot does not boil; Linguini mimes laughing.)

Nothing's happening. Maybe I didn't get the words right.

Bubble, bubble, pasta pot.
Make me noodles, nice and hot.
Pasta cooked 'til it's just right
Is perfect pasta, every strand.

(Pot does not boil.)

Still nothing? Let me think. *(pause)* Okay, I think I've got it!

Bubble, bubble, pasta pot.
Make me noodles, nice and hot.
Pasta cooked 'til it's just right
Is perfect pasta, every bite.

▶ *Pasta comes out of the pot. Luigi reacts with glee. Linguini shows concern. Carlo, Carmela, and Maria enter from stage right and go to the doorway.*

Carmela: Luigi, the pasta smells wonderful! I'm sorry that I doubted your cooking ability.

Maria: How did you cook so much pasta in such a short time?

Carlo: How does that pot cook without being on a stove?

Luigi: It's a magic pasta pot!

Carmela: Come on, Luigi, there's no such thing as a magic pasta pot.

Maria: Whatever! My headache's gone and I'm starving. Please pile some pasta onto my plate, Luigi.

▶ *Luigi serves the group and goes back into the house.*
Friends sit on the floor of the staging area and mime eating.

Luigi: *(calling from the doorway)* Do you want more pasta, Maria?

Maria: No, thank you, Luigi. It was so good, but I'm very full.

Carlo: I'm almost full, too, Luigi. You probably shouldn't make any more pasta.

Luigi: You're right. We seem to have enough pasta.
(goes back inside) Now, what were the words that Bella Nona said to stop the pot? *(pause)* Oh yes!

Please stop cooking, pasta pot.
I have noodles, nice and hot.
Your perfect pasta is the best.
Now it's time for you to rest.

(Pasta keeps coming out of the pot.)

Maybe I should have said "pasta perfect" instead of "perfect pasta." I'll try that.

Please stop cooking, pasta pot.
I have noodles, nice and hot.
Your pasta perfect is the best.
Now it's time for you to rest.

(Pot does not stop.)

What? Stop, pot, stop! I forbid you to make any more pasta!

▶ *Linguini points to the pot and makes the kissing motion.*
Luigi doesn't notice and runs out the doorway in a panic.

Maria: Is something wrong, Luigi?

Luigi:	Help me! I can't get the pot to stop making pasta!
Carmela:	*(smirking)* Why don't you use your magic?
Luigi:	My magic is failing me, and so is the pot!
Carlo:	Well, there has to be a knob or something somewhere to turn it off. *(enters the house, checks the pot, and comes out again)* Nope. Not a knob or a switch anywhere.

▶ *Sergio and Gina enter stage left; pasta is now coming out through the doorway.*

Sergio:	What's going on, Luigi? Why is there pasta all over the street?
Luigi:	I can't stop the pot! I don't know what to do!
Carmela:	You said the pot is magic, right, Luigi?
Luigi:	Yes! Right!
Carmela:	Tell us how it works. Then maybe we can help.
Luigi:	I say the magic words, and the pot makes perfect pasta! Then I say more words, and the pot stops making pasta!
Sergio:	I know some magic words. Maybe I can get it to stop. *(goes into the house and shouts)* Abracadabra! Zippity do! We've had just about enough pasta from you! *(returns to the group)* I guess that didn't work. Does anyone else know any magic words?
Carmela:	How about *Stop, Sesame*?
Carlo:	*Alakazam*?
Gina:	*Presto chango*?
Maria:	*Hocus pocus*?

Luigi: No! No! None of those words will work! Oh, what am I going to do? Bella Nona will be furious with me. I will lose my job—and my free pasta!

Carmela: Look at all these noodles! We have to stop that pot somehow! Before we know it, the pasta will start wrapping around our ankles and carrying us away!

Carlo: I can see the headline on the front page of the newspaper: *Six Attacked by Wild Pasta*!

Maria: Or *Runaway Pasta Has Mind of Its Own*!

Gina: *Speedy Spaghetti Swallows City*?

Sergio: What a mess you've gotten us into, Luigi! You and your magic pasta pot!

Gina: There's no time to point fingers, Sergio. We have to keep this spaghetti from spreading. Grab as much as you can, and let's throw it into a cart or something.

▶ *Linguini paces frantically.* **Bella Nona** *hobbles in from stage left (without potion).*

Bella Nona: *(stopping stage left of the doorway)* What's going on? Is that pasta I see flowing out of my house?

Luigi: *(meekly)* Yes, Bella Nona.

Bella Nona: Luigi! Did you touch the pasta pot?

Luigi: Oh no! I didn't touch the pot.

▶ *Linguini meows; points paw at mouth and then at Luigi.*

Bella Nona: *(nodding to Linguini)* I see. *(addressing Luigi)* Did you speak to the pot, Luigi?

Luigi: Oh dear … Yes, Bella Nona. I heard you speaking to the pot, so I said the words, too. But … but … I also said the words to make the pot stop! It just wouldn't listen! It seems to have a mind of its own!

Bella Nona: I understand the problem now, Luigi. If I can get through all this pasta, I will stop the pot.

Luigi: Thank you, Bella Nona. Here, let me help you.

► *Luigi* *helps Bella Nona through the doorway and then steps back and stands outside the doorway with the others.*

Bella Nona: Please stop cooking, pasta pot.
I have noodles, nice and hot.
Your perfect pasta is the best.
Now it's time for you to rest.

*(Bella Nona presses the fingertips of her right hand to her lips and throws a kiss to the pasta pot. **Linguini** mimics the kiss.)*

Mmmoi!

(The pot stops.)

Luigi: A kiss?

Bella Nona: Yes, Luigi. You must always show gratitude for the pasta that the pot provides.

Luigi: I'm sorry, Bella Nona, for breaking your trust. Forgive me, please, and give me another chance to work for you.

Bella Nona: You meant no harm, Luigi, so I will give you one more chance, but you must promise never to speak to the pasta pot again.

Luigi: I promise, Bella Nona. And I will never break this promise.

Carmela: Now what do we do with all this pasta?

The Magic Pasta Pot **43**

Carlo: Hand Luigi a fork and make him dig in?

▶ *Luigi* panics. Then *everyone* laughs.

Sergio: He would need a pitchfork!

Bella Nona: I have a better idea. Go round up all the dogs and cats in the neighborhood and bring them to a pasta party. They will have this street clean in no time.

Luigi: Yes, yes! Even our pets will enjoy Bella Nona's perfect pasta—pasta perfecto!

                          (*Linguini* licks his lips and rubs his tummy.)

▶ *All* except Bella Nona and Luigi hurry away with excitement. *Carlo* and *Carmela* exit stage left. *Sergio*, *Gina*, and *Maria* exit stage right. *Luigi* and *Bella Nona* exit stage left at a slower pace, ad-libbing conversation. *Linguini* prances along behind them.

What Is an Elephant?

Six blind people each inspect just one part of an elephant and come up with a limited understanding of what an elephant is. Only when they start putting their thoughts together do they see the big picture.
(Approximate running time: 11 minutes)

How to Prepare 46

How to Stage. 48

How to Wrap a Sari and a Turban 50

The Program 51

The Script 52

The Elephant Prop Sections 129–143

How to Prepare

INTRODUCE
the Story

Tell students that this play includes lines from the 19th-century American poem "The Blind Men and the Elephant," written by John Godfrey Saxe. The poem is easy to find on the Internet. Read the poem to the students and explain that it is based on an ancient fable from India. Remind the students that a fable is a story that teaches a lesson and invite them to discuss what the lesson is in the poem.

INTRODUCE
the Characters

Tell students that because the original story comes from India, the characters have Indian names. Write the names on the board and model pronouncing them. *(See the pronunciations below.)* Talk about Kamini's role as the storyteller and ask students to suggest how someone who has never been able to see might respond to a story about elephants.

INTRODUCE
the Script

Reproduce the script for each student. Before distributing the copies, review who the characters are and explain the role of the chorus. Then distribute the scripts for the students to read aloud. Do not assign roles at this point, but make sure that all students have an opportunity to read some of the play. During the reading, have the students ignore the stage directions, which are printed in italics.

CAST
the Roles

Assign the roles to best suit the size of your class and the abilities of your students. Here are some suggestions for casting:

1. When casting the role of Kamini, keep in mind that she interacts with the audience at times.

2. Having the six blind characters wear sunglasses may make playing an onstage role more comfortable for students who are not typically outgoing but who might perform very well behind the "safety" of the glasses.

3. The students playing the blind characters must be able to convey a lack of sight in other ways besides just wearing sunglasses. One way is by not directly facing anyone onstage who is speaking to them or to whom they are speaking.

4. You may include as many students as you wish in the chorus. If memorizing an adaptation of a 19th-century poem seems too challenging for the chorus members, have them read their lines instead of reciting them.

The Cast
(in order of appearance)

Kamini (*kuh•mee•nee*)

Maya (*my•uh*)

Ravi (*rah•vee*)

Hamid (*hah•meed*)

Tara (*tar•uh*)

Bala (*bah•luh*)

Sanji (*sahn•jee*)

Chorus

PRACTICE
the Lines

After assigning the roles, have students highlight their lines in their individual scripts. Then guide them through the script again, with each student reading his or her own character's lines.

After this reading, have students practice their lines as often as possible, both individually and as a group. Model expression and intonation to help them gain fluency and develop their characters' personalities.

As fluency improves, have the students playing the blind characters start walking single file, as described in the script, and practicing how to stand together and take their turns touching the elephant puzzle. Make sure that the cast members understand the characteristics of people who are vision-impaired and guide them to portray the blind characters with dignity.

Guidelines for Practicing

- Set a deadline date for having the lines memorized.
- Schedule classroom time for students to practice their lines.
- Encourage students to practice their lines at home.
- When the students seem confident reciting their lines, help them add movements and facial expressions that suit the characters and dialogue and are easy to perform in the staging area.

REHEARSE
the Play

1. Decide the location of the staging area early in the practice period, and encourage students to sit in the staging area even when they are just practicing their lines.

2. As soon as cast members know their lines, familiarize them with the staging area. Begin by showing them how the play's three locations are represented and where the chorus will stand throughout the play.

3. Refer to the script for suggested stage directions as to when and where characters will move. Adjust the directions to suit your staging area and your students' abilities. Suggest that the students playing the blind characters try rehearsing their movements with their eyes closed to give them an idea of how a person without sight might make those movements.

4. Rehearse the play in small sections. Go on to a new section only when cast members are comfortable with when and where they are supposed to move.

How to Stage

SET
the Stage

Designate an area of your classroom as "the stage." The action in the play takes place at three locations set closely together:

- the home of the blind characters (center stage)
- the mango tree (upstage right)
- the Rajah's palace (upstage left)

Displaying a large drawing of a green, leafy tree at stage right and the assembled sections of the elephant *(pages 129 to 143)* at stage left is an easy way to establish the onstage locations of the mango tree and the Rajah's palace.

Use the diagram below as a guide for positioning the cast and chorus at the start of the play.

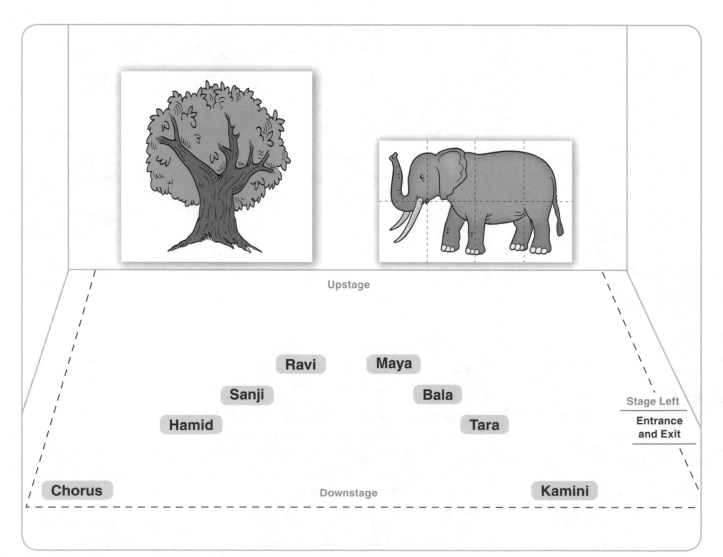

Upstage

Ravi   Maya

Sanji   Bala

Hamid   Tara

Stage Left

Entrance and Exit

Chorus   Downstage   Kamini

GATHER
the Props

The only prop needed for this play is an elephant for the blind characters to touch. A full-color elephant that can be pieced together and displayed quickly and easily is provided on pages 129 through 143.

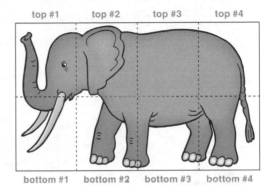

To assemble the prop, look at the number and location (top or bottom) on the back of each section and arrange the sections in numerical order from left to right.

If possible, laminate each section for added durability and ease of use. Attach double-sided tape to the backs of the sections to display them. Position the elephant at a height that is low enough for the actors to reach without stretching but high enough for the audience to see.

You might also wish to have each student who is playing a blind character wear a pair of sunglasses. The styles and colors of the sunglasses should be similar, or identical if possible, and plain enough that they do not distract the audience.

ASSEMBLE
the Costumes

No special costumes are necessary, but to help students develop their characters, two simple costume pieces are suggested:

- a sari (for each female character)
- a turban (for each male character)

Instructions for easy-to-make saris and turbans are provided on page 50. If possible, have each girl wear a sari of a different color or pattern.

At your discretion, chorus members may also wear saris and turbans or you may choose to just have them dress in clothes of a similar color or style.

It's Showtime!

The lines are memorized… The stage is set…
Now use the reproducible program on page 51
to announce the performance and introduce the cast!

How to Wrap a Sari and a Turban

The Sari

1 Drape a long scarf over the left shoulder so that the ends hang at equal lengths in front and in back.

2 Pull the front and back sides of the scarf diagonally to the right and pin the outside edges together near the bottom.

The Turban (Style #1)

1 Fold a 22- to 24-inch (56- to 61-cm) square of cloth (or use a large bandana) in half diagonally to form a triangle.

2 Fold up about 2 inches (5 cm) on the long side of the triangle.

3 Place the folded edge of the triangle at the top of the forehead, with the fold facing outward. (The point of the cloth should be hanging down at the back of the head.) Bring the ends around to the back of the head and tie them in a knot over the point. If the point is long enough, bring it up and tuck it in behind the knot.

The Turban (Style #2)

1 Drape a towel or a piece of cloth, 36 inches (91 cm) long and 12 inches (30 cm) wide, over the head. Twist the hanging ends until a kind of cap forms on the head.

2 Bring the ends around to the back and cross them low behind the head. Bring the ends back around to the front and cross them high over the forehead.

3 Bring the ends to the back again and tie a knot low on the head. Tuck any material still hanging into the cross folds.

Class: _____

presents the play

What Is an Elephant?

Starring

Kamini _____

Maya _____

Ravi _____

Hamid _____

Tara _____

Bala _____

Sanji _____

Chorus _____

_____

_____

_____

_____

_____

What Is an Elephant?

At the start of the play, all of the blind characters are sitting cross-legged in a semicircle at center stage. **Ravi**, **Hamid**, and **Sanji** sit together on the stage-right side of the semicircle; **Maya**, **Bala**, and **Tara** are on the stage-left side. **Kamini** stands downstage, left of center, positioned to address the audience. The **chorus** stands downstage, in the far-right corner.

Kamini: *(addressing the audience)* Welcome to India. My name is Kamini. I am a storyteller. Each week, I meet with my six friends. *(indicates the six)* All have been blind since birth. I tell them tales to stimulate their imaginations and to share with them the wonders of the world they have never seen.

▶ *Kamini turns away from the audience and walks upstage, stopping at the stage-left side of the semicircle.*

Kamini: Greetings, Maya, Bala, and Tara. *(Each woman smiles and slightly bows her head when her name is spoken.)* I trust that you women are well today.

Maya: Yes, Kamini, we are well, and we are happy that you are here with us.

Kamini: Greetings also to you, Ravi, Hamid, and Sanji. *(Each man smiles and slightly bows his head when his name is spoken.)* And you men are well, too?

Ravi: Good morning, Kamini. We are well, indeed.

Hamid: And we are anxious to hear the tale you have to share with us today.

Kamini: I want to tell you about my latest adventure. Shall we go outside and sit under the mango tree? The weather is beautiful today, my friends. Tara, here is my hand. *(puts Tara's hand in hers)* Today, you are the leader.

▶ *Tara stands; Kamini turns her to face stage right.*

Tara: Thank you, Kamini. Come, everyone, walk behind me and keep your right hand on the right shoulder of the person in front of you. *(all others stand)*

Ravi: *(sounding annoyed)* Yes, Tara, we know how to follow. You don't have to remind us.

Tara: I am the leader, Ravi, so please heed my instructions. Bala, follow my voice and stand behind me.

▶ *Bala moves behind Tara and stands with her right hand on Tara's right shoulder and her left hand extended for Maya to find.*

Bala: And, Maya, you stand behind me.

▶ *Maya lines up as directed.*

Tara: Hamid, please join us.

▶ *Maya holds out her hand so Hamid can find her.*

Hamid: Grab my hand, Sanji, and stand behind me.

▶ *Sanji does as Hamid asks and then holds out his hand for Ravi to find. Ravi gets in line without instruction.*

Tara: Are you in line, Ravi?

Ravi: Yes, Tara.

Tara: Good. Then we are ready.

Kamini: Do you remember how many steps to take to reach the mango tree, Tara?

Tara: Ten steps will get us there.

► *Still holding Tara's hand, **Kamini** slowly walks stage right.*
*The **others** follow Tara in a line, with right hands on right shoulders.*

Tara: *(pauses after walking five steps)* Ah, the sun feels warm on my skin. *(walks five more steps)*

Kamini: We have reached the tree. Please sit and get comfortable.

► *All turn forward and sit down on the floor in front of the tree; **Kamini** is downstage from the others, sitting somewhat in profile to the audience.*

Sanji: We are eager to hear your adventure, Kamini.

Kamini: It was wondrous, Sanji! I have just returned from the Rajah's palace. There, I saw a magnificent elephant!

Hamid: Elephant? I have never heard the word *elephant*. What is an elephant? What is its purpose?

Kamini: Well, Hamid, some elephants are taken to the forests, where they are used to clear away trees to make room for buildings. Other elephants carry people on their backs. The Rajah's elephant will carry his daughter when she travels from the palace to the hills.

Hamid: Do elephants make a sound?

Kamini: Oh yes. Their sounds are as loud as trumpet blasts that shake the earth.

► *The **friends** react with awe, except **Sanji**, who shakes his head in disbelief.*

Bala: An elephant sounds very dangerous.

Tara: Oh no, Bala! An elephant must be gentle to carry the princess on its back. The Rajah would not let his dear daughter ride on anything dangerous.

Maya: I thought Kamini said that an elephant is a trumpet.

Ravi: No, Maya. Kamini said an elephant *sounds* like a trumpet. An elephant is a living creature. I have heard of such an animal. It can toss a man into the air and then spear him through the heart with its sharp horns.

Hamid: Where did you hear such a story? It is obvious from what Kamini says that an elephant is much like a large cow.

Sanji: Ha!

Maya: Why do you laugh, Sanji? What do you think?

Sanji: I think all of you are very foolish. I do not believe any of it. Elephants do not exist.

Bala: But of course they do, Sanji! Kamini said so.

Ravi: Pay no attention to Sanji, Bala. He knows nothing.

Sanji: Apparently, I know more than you do.

Kamini: Stop your bickering, please. I will take you all to where the Rajah keeps the elephant. Then you can find out for yourselves what an elephant is. Come. Follow me.

▶ *All* stand and the *friends* follow Kamini stage left to the elephant, walking single file with right hands on right shoulders and stopping when each is aligned with the part of the elephant that he or she will touch (from stage left to stage right: Bala–the tail; Ravi–the body; Hamid–the leg; Sanji–the ear; Maya–the tusk; Tara–the trunk).

Kamini: We have arrived at the Rajah's stables. If you turn your body to the left and take a step forward, you will be close to the elephant. Reach out and touch it gently.

► *All* turn left to face the puzzle. As the **chorus** recites its verses, each character listens for his or her name to step forward and mime appropriate actions. *Ravi* steps forward first; the **others** sit. *Kamini* stands at center stage, looking on.

Chorus: Ravi approached the elephant and, happening to fall against its broad and sturdy side, at once began to bawl …

Ravi: (*shouting fearfully*) Have mercy!
Why, the elephant is solid—like a wall!

► *Maya* stands when she hears her name and steps forward.

Chorus: Next, Maya touched the creature's tusk and cried …

Maya: What have I here? It's round and smooth and yet so sharp.
To me, it seems quite clear that this animal, the elephant, is pointed—like a spear!

Ravi: Don't be silly, Maya. It has no points at all!
I have touched it for myself, and I say it's like a wall.

Maya: Come here, Tara. Tell us what you think.
Is the elephant like a wall or like a spear?

► *Tara* stands and steps forward. *Maya* stands aside (without blocking Tara or Ravi)

Chorus: Tara felt the animal and, happening to take the squirming trunk into her hands, she discovered their mistake.

Tara: I say it's neither wall nor spear. It wiggles like a snake!

Ravi: How can that be? The elephant does not move, I tell you!
What do you feel, Hamid?

► *Hamid* stands and steps forward. *Ravi, Tara,* and *Maya* sit.

Chorus: Hamid stretched out his eager hands and touched the creature's knee.

Hamid: What this amazing beast is like is clear enough to me.
An elephant is round and very like a mighty tree!
Sanji, what do you feel? Do you agree with me?

► *Sanji stands and steps forward.* **Hamid** *sits.*

Chorus: Sanji caught the creature's ear as it waved past his hand.
Said he …

Sanji: This cannot be a tree, but name it? Yes, I can!
It is flat and moving back and forth. I say, it's like a fan.

Hamid: *(stands)* Moving? No, you're wrong, Sanji. Ravi and I
will swear that what we felt with our four hands is still
just standing there.

Bala: *(stands and steps forward to touch the elephant)*
Hush! I will settle this argument, once and for all.

Chorus: From her place behind the beast, Bala now began to grope
and came to grasp the swinging tail that fell within her scope.
What she felt was thin and bristly.

Bala: The elephant is like a rope!

► *Sanji and* **Bala** *move away from the elephant.* **Tara, Maya,** *and* **Ravi** *stand
and all the* **friends** *gesture vigorously in various directions as they debate.*

Ravi: No, no, no! An elephant is like a wall!

Tara: How can an elephant be like a wall? I felt it squirm
in my hands. It's like a snake, I tell you!

Hamid: It is not like a wall or a snake. The elephant is sturdy
and round like a tree.

Maya: It is like a spear! I have no doubt.

Sanji: The fact that we cannot agree means that I was right in the first place. There is no such thing as an elephant. This is all just a trick. Kamini must be trying to fool us.

Kamini: *(advancing slightly toward the others)* Listen to yourselves, my friends. How can each of you be so certain that you are right?

Hamid: Well, I don't suppose we can be certain.

Kamini: Of course you can't. Each of you touched only part of the elephant. You must put all your thoughts together to know what an elephant is.

Hamid: What part did I touch, Kamini? What part of the elephant is as large as a mighty tree?

Kamini: Its legs are as large as tree trunks, Hamid. But you felt only one leg. An elephant has four such legs.

Hamid: Four massive legs! It must have a very large body if it needs four immense legs.

Ravi: I must have touched its body. What I touched felt very large and very strong. It felt like a wall!

Kamini: You are both right. Elephants are large and strong. The elephant is the largest animal to walk the earth.

Bala: Oh my! We are in the presence of a powerful beast!

Maya: I think I touched one of the elephant's horns. If it makes a sound like a trumpet, then it must have horns. And yet, the horn I felt had a closed tip from which no sound could escape. If I had such a horn, I would use it to dig in the earth.

Kamini: That was not a horn you felt, Maya. That was a tusk.
It is one of the elephant's two long teeth. They are so long
that they stick out on the sides of the elephant's mouth.
And you are right to think that the tusks are good for digging.
The elephant uses its tusks for digging—and for fighting!

Sanji: Since this animal is very large, I suppose I touched one
of its ears. If so, I think I was right to say it was like a fan.
Ears that big can be used like fans to cool the elephant
in the blazing sun.

Bala: And where the sun blazes, there are many bugs.
I am guessing that the elephant has a long, bristly tail,
which, to me, felt like a rope.

Kamini: Yes, Bala, the elephant does have a long, bristly tail,
and it uses its tail to swat at bugs to drive them away.

Maya: This animal seems perfectly suited to our hot weather.

Kamini: Now you are getting a good idea of what an elephant is
really like.

Tara: What part did I touch, Kamini? I cannot imagine any part
of the animal that would feel like a snake.

Kamini: You felt the animal's nose, Tara. It is called a trunk.

Tara: Impossible! Why would any animal need a nose that is
long enough to reach the ground?

Kamini: The elephant's trunk is a very unusual nose, indeed.
With it, the elephant grasps clumps of grasses and leaves
to eat. To drink, the elephant slurps up water with its trunk
and blows the water into its mouth. An elephant's trunk is so
strong and powerful that it can yank trees out of the ground!

► *The **friends** line up again, right hands on right shoulders. As they say their remaining lines, Kamini leads them to center stage and then downstage left to exit.*

Ravi: So an elephant is more than a wall.

Maya: Or a spear.

Tara: Or a snake.

Hamid: Or a tree.

Sanji: Or a fan.

Bala: Or a rope.

Kamini: Precisely. An elephant is a grand and amazing animal.

► ***All** exit downstage left. **Kamini** immediately returns to her stage-left position at the start of the play.*

Kamini: *(addressing the audience)* In the weeks that have passed since we visited the Rajah's elephant, I have shared many more tales and adventures with my six friends, and I am happy to say that they are now careful listeners who do not jump to conclusions about what they hear. *(exits downstage left)*

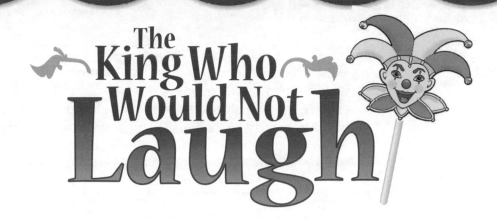

The King Who Would Not Laugh

A snooty king, who refuses to laugh or smile, comes up with a plan to reign forever. The king challenges his subjects to a contest he believes none of them can win. **(Approximate running time: 15 minutes)**

How to Prepare 62

How to Stage 64

How to Make the Pickle Spinner
   and the Fool's Scepter 66

The Program 67

The Script 68

The Masks and Props 145–161

How to Prepare

INTRODUCE
the Story

Tell students that this comedy is about a haughty king who is dethroned by his own court jester. Describe how the king challenges his subjects to make him laugh. To explore the plot further, ask questions such as: *Why would anyone choose not to laugh? What does the challenge tell you about the king? What problems might develop with such a challenge?*

INTRODUCE
the Characters

A good way to describe the characters in this play is to contrast the personalities of the arrogant king and his good-natured subjects. Make sure that all students know that the role of a jester, or fool, is to entertain a king and his court. Ask students to suggest things they might do to make someone laugh.

INTRODUCE
the Script

Reproduce the script for each student. Before distributing the copies, review who the characters are and explain the role of the storyteller as a narrator. Then distribute the scripts for the students to read aloud. Do not assign roles at this point, but make sure that all students have an opportunity to read some of the play. During the reading, have the students ignore the stage directions, which are printed in italics.

CAST
the Roles

All of the roles in this play are suitable for either girls or boys, but the demands of each role vary considerably. Assign the roles to best match the abilities of your students. Here are some suggestions for casting:

❶ The roles of the clowns, jokesters, and sillies are good for students who tend to be naturally energetic, high-spirited, and outgoing.

❷ The role of the king calls for a student who is capable of remaining serious while other characters are being silly. If you choose to cast a female, simply make the role a queen and change the pronouns in the script accordingly.

❸ Three roles are well-suited to students who are shy or have difficulty remembering lines and stage directions: The storyteller could read his or her lines rather than memorize them. The fool has a key role but with only a few lines and movements to remember. The king's servant has a nonspeaking role with easy, repetitive movements.

The Cast
(in order of appearance)

Storyteller	Cackles
Messenger	Chuckles
King	Zany
Bobo	Goofy
Bozo	Daffy
Boo-boo	Fool
Snickers	Servant

PRACTICE
the Lines

After assigning the roles, have students highlight their lines in their individual scripts. Then guide them through the script again, with each student reading his or her own character's lines.

After this reading, have students practice their lines as often as possible, both individually and as a group. Model expression and intonation to help them gain fluency and develop their characters' personalities.

As fluency improves, encourage the clowns, jokesters, and sillies to practice handling their props and adding actions and facial expressions to help individualize their characters. Let them have fun developing their roles, but provide enough guidance to keep onstage activity at an appropriate level. Direct students to deliver their lines, especially the jokes, slowly and distinctly enough to allow the audience to hear them clearly and enjoy the humor.

Guidelines for Practicing

• Set a deadline date for having the lines memorized.

• Schedule classroom time for students to practice their lines.

• Encourage students to practice their lines at home.

• When the students seem confident reciting their lines, help them add movements and facial expressions that suit the characters and dialogue and are easy to perform in the staging area.

REHEARSE
the Play

❶ Decide the location of the staging area early in the practice period and encourage students to sit in the staging area even when they are just practicing their lines.

❷ As soon as cast members know their lines, familiarize them with the staging area. Begin by showing them where they will enter and exit and where the storyteller will stand throughout the performance.

❸ Refer to the script for suggested stage directions as to when and where characters will move. Adjust the directions to suit your staging area and your students' abilities.

❹ Rehearse the play in small sections. Go on to a new section only when cast members are comfortable with when and where they are supposed to move.

How to Stage

SET
the Stage

Designate an area of your classroom as "the stage." The action of the play takes place in the king's castle and in three towns within the kingdom, but it is not necessary to divide the staging area into sections. You will need:

- 1 large chair *(for the king's throne)*, which is brought onstage about halfway through the play

Stick small pieces of masking tape on the floor of the staging area to indicate where to place the legs of the chair. Make sure that the position of the chair allows both the king and the characters performing in front of him to be seen by the audience.

Displaying a simple drawing or mural of a castle wall is an easy way to transform the staging area into a kingdom.

Use the diagram below as a guide for establishing entrances and exits and for positioning the storyteller, the king's throne, and the action in the towns.

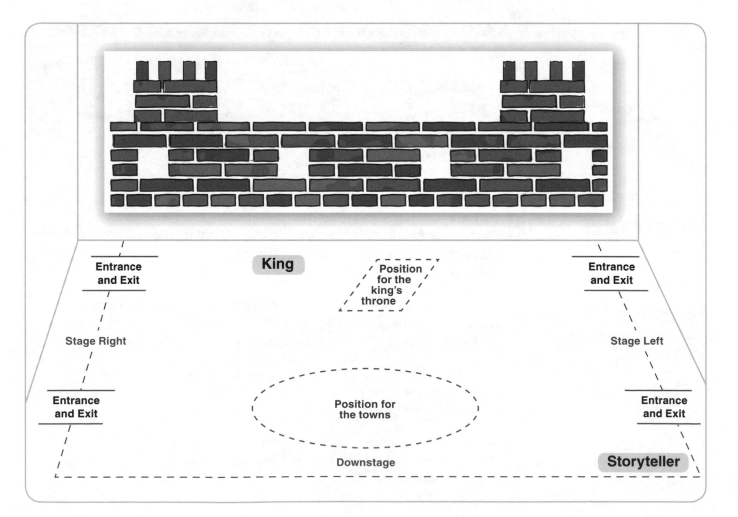

Entrance and Exit

King

Position for the king's throne

Entrance and Exit

Stage Right

Stage Left

Entrance and Exit

Position for the towns

Entrance and Exit

Downstage

Storyteller

GATHER
the Props

Using a few props in this play will enhance the performance and help characters recall their lines and movements. All of the props suggested below are easy to find or make and invite additional student participation. Note that several of the props are provided in this book.

- a large, impressive-looking book (*to hold the storyteller's script*)
- a paper scroll with the king's proclamation printed on it
- a kazoo (*for the messenger's trumpet*)
- Bozo's pickle spinner (*See pages 66 and 147.*)
- a pie tin and a 12- to 18-inch (30- to 46-cm) wooden stick or dowel (*for Bobo's balancing act*)
- Daffy's burger (*See page 159.*)
- Fool's scepter (*See pages 66 and 161.*)

ASSEMBLE
the Costumes

No special costumes are needed, but, at your discretion, some characters could wear distinguishing costume pieces, such as a brightly colored shirt, a funny wig or hat, or silly glasses. You might also allow the clowns, jokesters, and sillies to paint their faces in distinctive ways.

Costume Props

All script-related costume props, along with the instructions for making and wearing them, are provided in this book.

- Boo-boo's squirting flower (*See page 149.*)
- Bobo's oversized bow tie (*See page 151.*)
- Jokesters' badges (*See pages 153 and 155.*)

Masks

Full-color masks are provided for the king (*page 145*) and for Goofy (*page 157*). Directions for assembling the masks can be found on page 101.

It's Showtime!

The lines are memorized ... The stage is set ...
Now use the reproducible program on page 67
to announce the performance and introduce the cast!

How to Make...

The *Pickle Spinner*

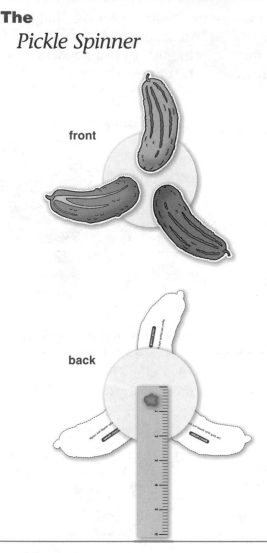

front

back

1 Cut out the three pickles on page 147. Laminate them, if possible, for added durability.

2 Cut an 8-inch (20-cm) circle out of white cardboard.

3 Glue the pickles onto the cardboard, spacing them evenly around the circle. Each pickle should extend beyond the circle. *(Use double-sided tape to attach the pickles if they are laminated.)*

4 Stick a pushpin through the center of the circle and into one end of a wooden ruler or paint-stirring stick. *(Do not push the pin tightly against the cardboard circle. The circle needs to be able to spin around on the pin.)*

5 If the point of the pushpin comes through the back of the ruler or paint stick, cover it completely with clay or putty or push a small eraser onto it to prevent injuries.

How to Use the Pickle Spinner

Holding the pickle spinner up and away from the body, grip the bottom end of the ruler in one hand and use one or two fingers of the other hand to spin the circle. As the pickles spin around like a pinwheel, the clown will appear to be juggling.

The *Fool's Scepter*

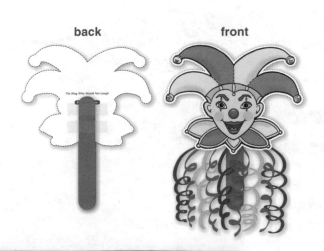

back   front

1 Cut out the fool's head on page 161. Laminate it, if possible, for added durability.

2 Use glue or tape to attach a large craft stick to the back of the cutout. Tape 2 to 3 inches (5 to 8 cm) of the craft stick to the bottom of the cutout, leaving about a 4-inch (10-cm) handle for manipulating the prop.

3 *(optional)* Tie multicolored streamers of thin ribbon or curling ribbon around the stick, under the cutout, to make the scepter look more festive.

Class: _____

presents the play

The King Who Would Not Laugh

Starring

Storyteller _____

Messenger _____

King _____

Bobo _____

Bozo _____

Boo-boo _____

Snickers _____

Cackles _____

Chuckles _____

Zany _____

Goofy _____

Daffy _____

Fool _____

Servant _____

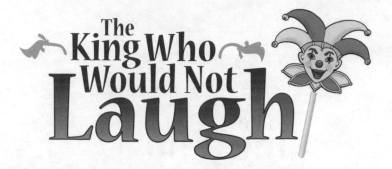

*At the start of the play, **King** is standing upstage right in an arrogant pose (nose in the air). **Storyteller** is positioned downstage, far left, and remains there throughout the play.*

Storyteller: There once lived a king who was very snooty.
His nose was always in the air. Being such a snob,
the king did not laugh—ever! He never even smiled.

► *Messenger enters upstage right and bows before the king.*

Messenger: You summoned me, Your Highness?

King: Yes, Messenger. Is it true that my subjects speak ill of me?

Messenger: There has been some talk, Sire.

King: I want you to tell me exactly what is being said.

Messenger: Well, Sire … *(nervously clears throat)* They say that your nose
is so high in the air it will one day get stuck in a cloud.

King: What? I don't believe it! What else are they saying?

Messenger: Er, uh … I have heard some refer to Your Highness as
King Picklepuss.

King: How dare they! Is that all?

Messenger: Some wonder if you suck on sour pickles all day long.

King: So they would prefer a king who laughs and tells jokes?

Messenger: So it seems, Sire.

King: Ha! I'd like to see any of them match my excellence as a ruler. *(jokingly)* Perhaps a subject who can make me laugh should rule the kingdom.

Messenger: Are you proclaiming a contest, Your Highness?

King: A contest? Why, no … I mean, yes! *(smiles deviously)* Yes— a contest I am sure to win. Messenger! I command you to ride to every hill, dale, nook, and cranny of my kingdom and announce that whoever can make the king laugh shall henceforth rule the kingdom.

Messenger: *(bows)* As you wish, Your Highness.

King: Come with me. I shall draw up the proclamation.
*(**King** and **Messenger** exit upstage right.)*

► *Messenger enters downstage right with a scroll and mimes riding a horse; stops downstage center.*

Storyteller: With the king's proclamation in hand, the messenger set off on horseback. He soon arrived at a tiny town filled with tricycles, tiny cars, and whipped-cream pies. The place was called Clown Town. The messenger sounded his trumpet. *(blows a kazoo)* Three clowns named Bobo, Bozo, and Boo-boo came quickly.

► *Bobo, Bozo, and Boo-boo enter downstage left.*

Bobo: What's the king's messenger doing in Clown Town, Bozo?

Bozo: Ya got me, Bobo. But you can be sure that any news coming from King Picklepuss isn't good news.

Messenger: Hear ye! Hear ye! Hear ye!
Because the king is a friendly and considerate ruler …

Boo-boo: *(as an aside)* Ha! That's a laugh!

Messenger: ... His Royal Highness has asked me to make this proclamation: *(reads the proclamation with importance)* *Whoever can make the king laugh shall henceforth rule the kingdom. All interested subjects must report to the castle on April first.*

▶ *Messenger exits downstage left.*

Bobo: Well, that'll sure be easy for us, eh, Bozo?

Bozo: It sure will, Bobo. And I know just what I'm going to do. Because the king seems to love pickles so much, I'm going to juggle some of those slippery little things. That'll make the king laugh his crown off!

Boo-boo: Well, I'm going to need one of the squirting posies from my flower garden. There's nothing like a squirting flower to get a good laugh. What's your plan, Bobo?

Bobo: I could make funny balloon animals, but my three-legged pig still needs a little work. I think maybe I'll perfect my balancing act instead.

▶ *Clowns mime conversation as they exit downstage right.*
Messenger enters upstage left and moves to downstage center.
Snickers, Cackles, and Chuckles enter downstage left.

Storyteller: The king's messenger rode on through the forest and across the meadow and soon arrived at a village called Joke Town. Once again, the messenger blew his trumpet. *(blows a kazoo)* Snickers, Cackles, and Chuckles were the first jokesters to gather 'round.

Messenger: Hear ye! Hear ye! Hear ye!
Because the king is a friendly and considerate ruler ...

Snickers: *(as an aside)* Ha! That's a joke!

Messenger:	… His Royal Highness has asked me to make this proclamation: *(reads the proclamation with importance)* *Whoever can make the king laugh shall henceforth rule the kingdom. All interested subjects must report to the castle on April first.*

► *Messenger exits downstage left.*

Cackles:	*(to Snickers and Chuckles)* I guess you two had better get used to calling me King Cackles. I've got some knock-knock jokes that are sure to win me the throne. Here's a good one! "Knock, knock."
Snickers:	All right, Cackles. I'll play along. "Who's there?"
Cackles:	"Champ."
Snickers:	"Champ who?"
Cackles:	"Champ who your hair. It's dirty!" Ha! Ha! Ha!
Chuckles:	Not so fast, Cackles! My riddles are a lot funnier than your knock-knock jokes. Listen to this one. It'll have the king rolling in the courtyard. "Why did the cookie go to the doctor?"
Cackles:	I give up. Tell me.
Chuckles:	"Because he was feeling crummy!" Ha! Ha! Ha!
Snickers:	Not bad, Chuckles, but not as good as my frog jokes. Here's one of my favorites. "Why are frogs always happy?" *(pause)* Give up? "They eat whatever bugs 'em!" Ha! Ha! Ha!
Cackles:	That *was* pretty funny, Snickers. I'd say at least one of us is sure to make the king laugh.
Snickers:	And his crown is gonna look mighty good on *me*!

► *Snickers, Cackles, and Chuckles mime laughter and conversation as they exit downstage right.*

► *Zany, Goofy, and Daffy enter upstage left (guffawing and acting silly) and move to downstage center. Messenger enters downstage left and crosses to center.*

Storyteller: The messenger rode on to the last village in the kingdom. It was called Silly Town. When he arrived, three sillies named Zany, Goofy, and Daffy were there to greet him— but he sounded his trumpet anyway. *(blows a kazoo)*

Messenger: Hear ye! Hear ye! Hear ye!
Because the king is a friendly and considerate ruler ...

Zany: *(as an aside)* Ha! That's the silliest thing I've ever heard!

Messenger: ... His Royal Highness has asked me to make this proclamation: *(reads the proclamation with importance)*
Whoever can make the king laugh shall henceforth rule the kingdom. All interested subjects must report to the castle on April first.

► *Messenger exits downstage right.*

Goofy: Goody, goody, goody! I'll finally have a chance to try out my new silly faces.

Zany: Like the one where you squirt milk out of your mouth while you wiggle your ears?

Goofy: My new ones are even sillier than that, Zany.

Zany: Well, I've been practicing the silliest sneeze you ever heard. It'll blow the king right off his throne. *Ah ... aah ... aaah ... CHOOOOOOO!*

Daffy: That was some sneeze, Zany. It made the ground shake!

► *Zany, Goofy, and Daffy continue talking and laughing as they exit downstage right.*

Goofy: Are you going to sing one of your silly songs, Daffy?

Daffy: Probably. What do you think of this one?
(sings to the tune of "Baa, Baa, Black Sheep")
Chocolates are a yum yum ve-ge-tay-ble.
I always eat as many as I am a-ble.

Goofy: I like it! I like it! *(slaps knee and guffaws)*

Zany: *(doubling over with laughter)* Me, too! Me, too!

▶ *Messenger enters upstage right with the* **Fool**, *stopping halfway to upstage center.*

Storyteller: When the messenger returned to the castle, he showed the proclamation to the fool.

Messenger: At the king's command, I have delivered this proclamation hither and yon. *(reads from the scroll)* *Whoever can make the king laugh shall henceforth rule the kingdom. All interested subjects must report to the castle on April first.*

Fool: *(with a sly smile)* I see.

▶ *Fool exits upstage left.* **Storyteller** *speaks over commotion as* **Clowns**, **Jokesters**, *and* **Sillies** *enter upstage right and line up at stage right.* **Fool** *enters upstage left, places a chair (king's throne) upstage center, and then joins the others at stage right.* **King** *and* **Servant** *enter upstage right.* **King** *sits on the throne.* **Servant** *stands stage left of throne.* **Messenger** *stands stage right of throne.*

Storyteller: On April first, three clowns, three jokesters, three sillies, and a fool came to the castle. The king greeted them with a sour look. Although he felt certain that no one could make him laugh, he did not want to risk losing his throne, so he had sucked on sour pickles all morning, just to be safe.

King: Let's get on with it. Messenger, read the rules.

Messenger: Hear ye! Hear ye! *(reads from the scroll)* *You will each have one—and only one—chance to make the king laugh. If no one makes the king laugh, the king shall reign forever.* Bozo the Clown, please step forward.

Bozo: *(steps up to the throne with pickle spinner prop behind him)* Your Majesty *(bows)*, for your entertainment, I will juggle some things that I hear you like very much.

▶ *Bozo spins the pickles;* ***Messenger*** *reacts with shock.*

King: *(enraged)* So you are the knave who calls me King Picklepuss! Off to the dungeon with you!

▶ ***Servant*** *takes Bozo's arm, leads him out through the upstage-left exit, and then returns to the stage.*

Messenger: Bobo the Clown is next, Sire.

Bobo: Your Highness *(bows)*, you're gonna love my balancing act! *(tries to balance a pie plate on a stick on his nose)*

▶ ***Messenger*** *reacts with surprise.* ***King*** *is angry.*

King: How dare you mock me with your nose in the air. *(points stage left)* Off to the dungeon with you!

▶ ***Servant*** *removes a reluctant Bobo and then returns to the stage.*

Messenger: Now here is Boo-boo the Clown.

Boo-boo: Your Majesty *(bows)*, let me just say …

King: Just begin, clown!

Boo-boo: As you wish, Your Highness. If it pleases Your Majesty, I will need the assistance of your Messenger.

▶ ***King*** *nods his approval. Bewildered* ***messenger*** *approaches Boo-boo.*

Boo-boo: *(pointing to the flower prop)* I have grown a special flower just for this occasion. Please smell it, Messenger, to be sure that it is fragrant enough for a king.

Messenger bends toward the flower, and ***Boo-boo*** *mimes squirting him in the face.* *Clowns,* ***jokesters****, and* ***sillies*** *laugh hilariously.*

King: *(furiously)* I see no humor in misusing a flower to play nasty tricks! *(Laughter stops abruptly; King points toward the dungeon.)* Off to the dungeon with you!

▶ *Servant removes a crying Boo-boo and then returns to the stage.*

Messenger: Next, please. *(Snickers steps forward.)* This is Snickers, Your Highness. He's from Joke Town.

Snickers: I am honored to be here, Your Majesty. *(bows)* My jokes are sure to make you laugh. Listen to this one. "What happened to the frog who parked at a bus stop?" *(pause)* "He got toad away!" *(laughs hilariously)*

Messenger: Oh dear! I didn't know that Snickers would joke about your favorite amphibian, Sire!

King: *(pointing toward the dungeon)* Off to the dungeon with you!

▶ *Servant removes a surprised (but still laughing) Snickers and then returns to the stage.*

Messenger: Perhaps this next jokester will not be as offensive, Your Highness. His name is Chuckles.

Chuckles: *(bowing)* You will be relieved to know, Your Majesty, that I have no jokes to tell. I have riddles! Allow me to begin. *(clears throat)* "What vegetable do you get when King Kong walks through your garden?" Give up? "Squash!" *(waits for laughter)*

King: I do not know this King Kong, but how dare you make fun of any king! Off to the dungeon with you!

Chuckles: But … but, Sire! King Kong isn't a real king! He's just called "King" because he's so big!

▶ *Servant removes a protesting Chuckles and then returns to the stage.*

Messenger: The last jokester, Your Highness, is Cackles.

Cackles:	Your Most Royal Highness *(bows)*, please allow me to present my finest joke.
King:	*(angrily)* Just get on with it!
Cackles:	Yes, Sire. "Knock, knock."
King:	What do you mean, "knock, knock"? That's the most ridiculous joke I've ever heard! You're not even near a door! *(points toward the dungeon)* Off to the dungeon with you!

► *Servant leads Cackles away.*

Cackles:	*(calling back to the king)* No, wait! That's just the beginning! You're supposed to say "Who's there?" Stop! This is unfair! *(Servant returns to the stage alone.)*
Messenger:	And now, Your Highness, here is a Silly named Zany.
Zany:	*(bows with exaggerated arm motions)* Your Royalness, for your laughing pleasure, I … *ah … ah … ah … CHOOOOOO!*

► *All react as if the sneeze has sprayed them. King is flabbergasted. Messenger pretends to wipe the sneeze off the king's face.*

Storyteller:	Zany gave the sneeze of a lifetime, his silliest sneeze ever. But it sprayed everywhere!
King:	*(speaking through the messenger's handkerchief)* That's not funny! Are you trying to make me sick? Off to the dungeon with you!

► *Servant leads Zany to the dungeon.*

Zany:	I'm so sorry, Sire. I didn't mean to spray you. That was my silliest sneeze ever! Didn't you think it was at least a little funny? *(Servant returns to the stage alone.)*
Messenger:	Here's another Silly, Sire. This is Daffy.

Daffy: *(bows)* Your Royal Royalness, I invite you to enjoy my silly song. *(sings a few notes to prepare his voice and then sings to the tune of "On Top of Spaghetti")* On top of a burger, all covered with cheese, I lost all my ketchup, when somebody sneezed.

King: What! You knew about the sneeze? You knew about it and just let your Silly friend sneeze all over me? Off to the dungeon with you! Your song is disgusting!

Daffy: But you'll love the next verse, Your Highness! I guarantee that it will make you laugh.

▶ *Servant leads Daffy to the dungeon and then returns to the stage.*

Messenger: The last Silly is Goofy, Your Highness.

Goofy: *(bows)* Your Most Royal Royalness, I have a remarkable face that is certain to make you laugh.

▶ *As **Goofy** makes a silly face, **King** falls asleep and snores.*

Messenger: Your Majesty, Goofy is making a face at you. *(shouts)* Sire?

▶ *King awakens with a start.*

King: Huh? *(regaining awareness)* You're making a face at me! I will not tolerate such disrespect! Off to the dungeon with you!

▶ *Servant leads Goofy offstage and then returns to the stage.*

Messenger: Only the fool remains, Sire. His will be the final attempt to make Your Highness laugh.

Fool: *(bows but keeps eyes fixed on the king)* Your Majesty, permit me to say that I believe there is a reason you do not laugh.

King: Is that so? Pray, tell me what that reason is.

Fool: The reason is simple. You do not know *how* to laugh.

King: How foolish! Of course I know how to laugh!

Fool: Pardon me for saying so, but if Your Majesty could laugh, Your Majesty surely would. I do not think that you are capable of laughing.

King: Preposterous! I *can* laugh, I tell you!

Fool: Does Your Majesty make a claim that he does not prove? Prove that you can laugh, Your Highness.

▶ *King mimes what the storyteller describes.*

Storyteller: Not one to back away from a challenge, the king took a deep breath and, with all his might, forced his mouth into a grin. Almost instantly, the grin turned into a giggle, and moments later, the king was laughing so hard that he fell off his throne.

Messenger: Pardon me. *(removes the king's mask and puts it on the fool; Fool sits on the throne)* Hail to the king!

Fool: *(addressing the former king)* As you have just seen, I am no fool when it comes to fooling. But please rise now. *(King stands, still chuckling.)* To honor your long service to this kingdom, I wish to appoint you to the most important position in my royal court. *(handing his scepter to the king)* Henceforth, you shall be my court jester. Your job will be to help all subjects smile and laugh every day.

King: It will be my pleasure, Your Majesty. I haven't had this much fun in years!

▶ *Fool stands and leads King, Messenger, and Servant off upstage right.*

Storyteller: And that, my friends, is how one hearty laugh toppled a king and brought a fool to the throne. *(exits downstage left)*

Dorothy in the Land of Blahs

*One minute, Dorothy is playing an exciting new arcade game with her friends. The next minute, she's with a batch of Bobs in a dull, gray place called Blahs, trying to tame a wicked witch and then find her way back home. **(Approximate running time: 17 minutes)***

How to Prepare 80

How to Stage...................... 82

How to Make Bob's Arrow 84

The Program 85

The Script 86

The Masks and Props......... 163–175

How to Prepare

INTRODUCE
the Story

Invite students to share what they know about the book or the movie *The Wizard of Oz*. Tell them that this play is a fractured and shortened version of the story, featuring Dorothy in a boring and colorless land controlled by the WWW (Wicked Witch of the Web). Explain that *Blahs* in the title of the play comes from the adjective *blah*, which means "boring," "lifeless," or "dull."

INTRODUCE
the Characters

Name and briefly describe the characters in the play and explain the role of the witch in creating Blahs. Help students understand the relationship of the characters to the setting by asking questions such as: *How would people in a place called Blahs act or dress? Why do you think they're all named Bob? How would Dorothy's friends act differently from the Bobs in Blahs? How would you expect the witch to treat the people in Blahs? How would they feel toward her?*

INTRODUCE
the Script

Reproduce the script for each student. Before distributing the copies, review who the characters are and explain the roles of the narrators. Then distribute the scripts for the students to read aloud. Do not assign roles at this point, but make sure that all students have an opportunity to read some of the play. During the reading, have the students ignore the stage directions, which are printed in italics.

CAST
the Roles

The Cast	
(in order of appearance)	
Narrator 1	Bob 1
Narrator 2	Witch
Dorothy	Bob 2
Ty	Bob 3
Tory	Rainbow 1
Tracy	Rainbow 2

Assign the roles to best suit the size of your class and the abilities of your students. Here are some suggestions for casting:

❶ Assign the role of Dorothy to a bubbly and enthusiastic girl, someone who can clearly bring cheer to the Land of Blahs.

❷ The Wicked Witch of the Web is a fun role that does not require much memorizing. It does, however, require an outgoing student who will relish playing "the bad guy."

❸ The three Bobs can be played by boys or girls or both. Casting a female as one or more of the Bobs can add even more fun to the play.

❹ The roles of Tracy, Ty, and Tory, as well as the students who carry the rainbow prop, can also be played by either boys or girls and offer good opportunities for shy students or English language learners to participate onstage. These characters have only a few lines or no lines at all to memorize and are in front of the audience for a relatively short period of time.

PRACTICE
the Lines

After assigning the roles, have students highlight their lines in their individual scripts. Then guide them through the script again, with each student reading his or her own character's lines.

After this reading, have students practice their lines as often as possible, both individually and as a group. Model expression and intonation to help them gain fluency and develop their characters' personalities.

As fluency improves, have the students start practicing with their props and encourage them to pay special attention to showing a distinct difference between the two settings in the play. Dorothy, Ty, Tory, and Tracy need to be particularly active and outgoing. In contrast, the three Bobs should initially be listless in speech and action and become increasingly more animated after Dorothy gives them their colorful apparel. Also, make sure that you allow plenty of time for Dorothy and the Bobs to practice giving the witch her makeover.

Guidelines for Practicing

- Set a deadline date for having the lines memorized.

- Schedule classroom time for students to practice their lines.

- Encourage students to practice their lines at home.

- When the students seem confident reciting their lines, help them add movements and facial expressions that suit the characters and dialogue and are easy to perform in the staging area.

REHEARSE
the Play

1 Decide the location of the staging area early in the practice period and encourage students to sit in the staging area even when they are just practicing their lines.

2 As soon as cast members know their lines, familiarize them with the staging area. Begin by showing them where they will enter and exit and where the narrators will stand throughout the play.

3 Refer to the script for suggested stage directions as to when and where characters will move. Adjust the directions to suit your staging area and your students' abilities.

4 Rehearse the play in small sections. Go on to a new section only when cast members are comfortable with when and where they are supposed to move.

How to Stage

SET
the Stage

Designate an area of your classroom as "the stage." The action takes place at an arcade that, with the flip of a sign, becomes the Land of Blahs and then becomes the arcade again. You will need:

- a long table
- a tablecloth or blanket that is large enough to fully cover the table
- a long, narrow bench (or 3 chairs or stools)
- a small table (or desk) with a computer monitor on it
- a chair *(for the witch to sit on)*

Displaying a simple drawing or mural of gray clouds hanging over gray silhouettes of trees, houses, and buildings is an easy way to transform the staging area into the Land of Blahs.

Use the diagram below as a guide for establishing entrances and exits and for positioning characters, set pieces, and props at the start of the play.

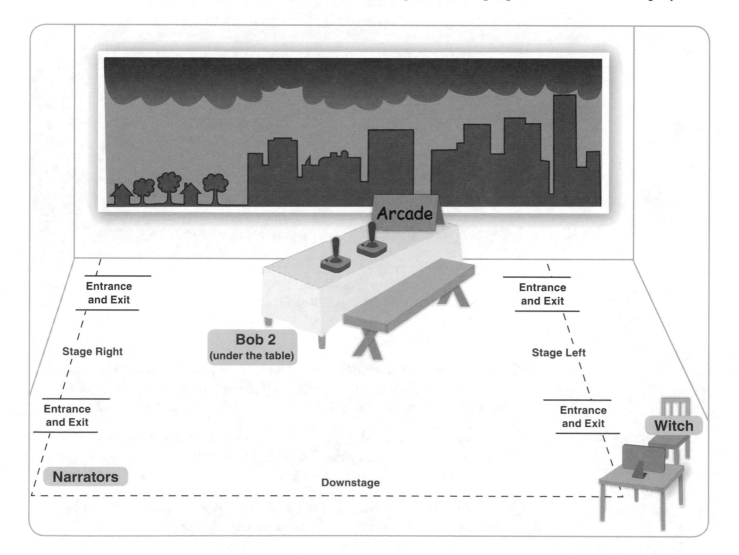

GATHER
the Props

Using a few key props will enhance the performance and help characters recall their lines and movements. All of the props suggested below are easy to find or make and invite additional student participation.

Arcade
- a two-sided sign (**Arcade** on one side; **Information** on the other)
- 2 joysticks

Dorothy
- a colorful tote bag with a shoulder strap
- *(inside the tote)* cellphone; brightly colored cap; pair of brightly patterned socks; long, brightly patterned scarf; curling iron; large, gaudy clip-on earrings; tiara; hand mirror

Bob 1
- a two-sided arrow *(See page 84.)*

Bob 3
- a cloth laundry bag (or a small duffel bag or backpack) with the Wonderful Witch mask *(page 165)* stored inside it

Witch
- magic wand *(See pages 167 and 169.)*

ASSEMBLE
the Costumes

No special costumes are needed, but students should try to incorporate the following color guidelines with their everyday attire: Dorothy should wear a variety of bright colors, the three Bobs should wear all gray, the witch should wear black, and the students playing the rainbow *(pages 171–175)* should wear as many colors of the rainbow as possible.

Masks
The student playing the witch will wear two masks during the play. As the Wicked Witch, she will wear the mask on page 163. After her makeover, she will wear the mask on page 165. The directions for assembling both full-color masks are on page 101.

It's Showtime!

**The lines are memorized… The stage is set…
Now use the reproducible program on page 85
to announce the performance and introduce the cast!**

How to Make Bob's Arrow

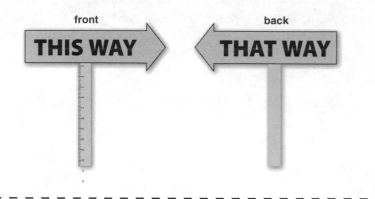

front

THIS WAY

back

THAT WAY

❶ Photocopy the arrow template on this page and cut it out along the dashed lines.

❷ Use the template to draw the point of the arrow on white or gray poster board. Extend the lines for the shaft of the arrow 10 inches (25 cm) to make the arrow 17 inches (43 cm) long from the tip. Then cut out the arrow.

❸ Repeat step 2 to make another arrow. The second arrow should be exactly the same size and shape as the first one.

❹ Lay one arrow flat on a table, with the tip pointing to the right, and use a thick black marker to print THIS WAY in big, bold letters.

❺ Lay the second arrow flat, with the tip pointing to the left, and write THAT WAY.

❻ Use strong tape to attach a ruler to the back of one arrow.

❼ Lay the other arrow back to back over the first arrow with the points at the same end. Use glue or double-sided tape to hold the arrows together.

THAT WAY

Class: _____

presents the play

Dorothy in the Land of Blahs

Starring

Narrator 1 _____

Narrator 2 _____

Dorothy _____

Ty _____

Tory _____

Tracy _____

Bob 1 _____

Bob 2 _____

Bob 3 _____

Witch _____

Rainbow 1 _____

Rainbow 2 _____

Dorothy in the Land of Blahs

*At the start of the play, the arcade is set upstage center, with **Bob 2** hiding under the table.*
*Narrator 1 and **Narrator 2** stand downstage, far right, and stay there throughout the play.*
***Witch** is sitting downstage, far left (slightly off the staging area), at a table with a computer monitor.*
(She can be seen and heard by the audience, but the actors appear unaware until she confronts them.)

▶ ***Dorothy** enters upstage right, happy and energetic as she mimes waiting for her friends.*

Narrator 1:	Dorothy Hale is a girl who is always on the go. She lives with her Aunt Em in Nome, Alaska. Aunt Em says that the way Dorothy whirls from one thing to another, she must have been born in a cyclone. Already today, Dorothy has practiced her tuba, made peanut butter cookies, taken books back to the library, and been to the shopping mall.
Narrator 2:	Aunt Em bought her a new tote bag. *(**Dorothy** admires her tote bag and rummages around in it.)* Dorothy carries a tote bag with her everywhere. "You never know when you're gonna need something," she says. So she keeps a little of everything in her tote.

▶ ***Ty** and **Tory** enter downstage right and wave to Dorothy. The three join at right center and mime conversation as they walk downstage (right to left) and then upstage (to center).*

Narrator 1:	Today, Dorothy is with her friends Ty and Tory. The day has turned gray and rainy, so they've decided to go to the arcade. Another friend, Tracy, is planning to meet them there.
Narrator 2:	So far, it's been a pretty ordinary Saturday, but knowing Dorothy, it probably isn't going to stay that way.
Tracy:	*(running in from upstage left)* Hey, guys! Sorry I'm late.
Dorothy and Ty:	Hi, Tracy!

Tory: It's about time! I thought you'd never get here.

Tracy: What's the rush?

Tory: I heard that the arcade has a new simulator, and I've been waiting all week to check it out. It's called a storm chaser. C'mon, let's go inside. (*All move toward the arcade props.*)

Ty: Look! (*points at the props*) There it is!

► *Ty and Tory rush to the bench. Tory sits on the upstage end.*
Ty sits on the downstage end and grabs a joystick.

Narrator 1: Tory wasted no time jumping into the simulator. Ty followed him and grabbed a controller joystick.

Dorothy: (*squeezing in between Ty and Tory and grabbing the other joystick*) Make room, you two! I'm gonna drive. Come on, Tracy. We can squeeze you in.

Tracy: (*yawning*) No thanks. Simulators are boring.

► *Dorothy, Ty, and Tory make whooshing (wind) sounds as they shake, lean, and jolt to mime operating the simulator. Tracy stands stage right of the props, looking on.*

Ty: Watch it, Dorothy! Don't get so close to the twister. You're making everything shake.

Dorothy: (*miming a struggle*) It's not me! It's the simulator!

Tory: (*stands*) Get up! I'll drive.

Dorothy: (*annoyed*) Whatever!

► *Dorothy and Tory mime stumbling around as they switch positions. (Whooshing sound gets louder.)*

Narrator 2: The noisy simulator's miniature car was shaking like a paint mixer, and as Dorothy was trying to switch seats with Tory, she lost her balance and tumbled onto the floor.

► **Dorothy** *mimes falling onto the floor (stage left of the arcade props). She sits on the floor, looking dazed, as **Tracy**, **Ty**, and **Tory** react with alarm and then freeze in position.*

Dorothy: *(stands unsteadily and twirls slowly downstage)*
Where am I? Why is everything spinning?

► **Tracy** *turns the "Arcade" sign to "Information" and exits upstage right. **Ty** and **Tory** exit upstage left, taking the joysticks with them. **Dorothy** twirls downstage right and sits on the stage floor, facing the audience and looking dazed.*

Narrator 1: When the spinning stopped, Dorothy found herself all alone. There was nothing around her but silence.

► **Bob 1** *enters downstage right (with arrow), coming only a few steps into the staging area.*

Narrator 2: Or so she thought.

Dorothy: *(looking around)* Tory? Ty? Where did everybody go?
I'll call Tracy. Where's my phone? *(rummages through her tote and pulls out a cellphone)* No signal? Well, that's just great!
(stands and looks around) I don't think I'm at the arcade anymore! *(takes a few steps backward and bumps into Bob 1)*

Bob 1: Ouch!

Dorothy: *(whirls around, startled)* Whoa! I didn't see you there!
(pauses briefly for a double take) Maybe because your gray shirt blends into the gray buildings that blend into the gray trees that blend into the gray sky that blends right back into you again. Where am I? Graysland?

Bob 1: *(yawning)* Nope.

Dorothy: Sleepy Hollow?

Bob 1: Huh?

Dorothy: Never mind. I'm Dorothy. Who are you?

Bob 1:   Bob.

Dorothy: Hi, Bob. Will you please tell me where I am?

Bob 1:   Blahs.

Dorothy: Blahs? As in *blah, blah, blah*?

Bob 1:   No, just one *blah*—with an *s* at the end.

Dorothy: I've never heard of Blahs. I'm from Nome … Nome, Alaska. Can you tell me how to get back home to Nome?

Bob 1:   I suppose you can go this way … *(turns arrow so "THIS WAY" faces forward)* or that way. *(turns arrow so "THAT WAY" faces forward)*

Dorothy: What's with the arrow?

Bob 1:   Isn't it obvious? It shows which way the road goes.

Dorothy: But why are you holding it?

Bob 1:   It's my job. I work for Blahs Transit.

Dorothy: You hold an arrow for Blahs Transit? *(brief pause)* All day long? *(brief pause)* Is that all you do?

Bob 1:   Yep.

Dorothy: Aren't you dying of boredom?

Bob 1:   Nope. *(pauses and then points arrow upstage)* Sometimes I get to change directions.

Dorothy: Yeah? Like that's a real pick-me-up! *(brief pause)* Are you going to hold that arrow for the rest of your life?

Bob 1:   *(yawning)* Guess so.

Dorothy: Do you ever want to do something else?

Bob 1: I think I'd like to be an engineer again. I used to design superhighways. But now, I just don't have the energy.

Dorothy: What happened to it?

Bob 1: My energy? It got zapped.

Dorothy: Zapped? How?

Bob 1: One minute, I'm on the Web, researching road surfaces. The next minute—Zzzzt! That WWW sure has a lot of power.

Dorothy: The World Wide Web zapped you?

Bob 1: Well, not exactly. It was the Wicked Witch of the Web.

Dorothy: The *who-what-which* of the *where*?

Bob 1: The *Wicked Witch* of the *Web*—the WWW. She controls the Web around here. She runs everything in Blahs.

Witch: *(cackling evilly)* Heh, heh, heh! And so I do!

Dorothy: Maybe she can tell me how to get back home to Nome. Where can I find this, uh … witch person?

Bob 1: She spends a lot of time in Sillycon Valley.

Dorothy: Does this road go to Sillycon Valley?

Bob 1: I don't know *where* the road goes. I only know *which way* it goes. Why do you ask?

Dorothy: Because we have to do something about this WWW!

Bob 1: *We*?

Dorothy: Yes, *we*. You want your energy back, don't you?
And I want to get back home to Nome. So come on, Bob!
We're off to see the Wicked Old Web-Witch of Blahs.

Bob 1: You mean, the Wicked Witch of the Web.

Dorothy: Whatever!

Narrator 1: Dorothy took Bob by the arm, and off they went
down the black asphalt road ...

Narrator 2: ... Dorothy with her tote bag and Bob with his arrow.

► *Dorothy* and *Bob 1* walk arm in arm upstage.

Bob 1: Ah ...ahhh ...ah-CHOO!

Dorothy: Are you catching a cold, Bob? I wouldn't be surprised.
It's awfully damp here in Blahs. *(pulls a colorful cap out of her tote)*
Here! Put on this cap to keep your head warm.

Witch: *(throwing up her hands and shrieking)* No, Bob! The colors! Stop!

Bob 1: *(puts on the cap)* Thanks! This feels much better.

Witch: *(scowling and muttering)* Curses! Bob's not so blah anymore.

► *Dorothy* and *Bob 1* reach the information station (upstage center).

Dorothy: Look, Bob! Information. Just what we need.
Hello? Is anybody here?

Bob 2: *(pops out from under the table)*
(speaking rudely) What do you want?

Dorothy: There's no need to be rude. My friend and I want
some information. Would you please tell us how
to get to Sillycon Valley?

Bob 2:	Nope. Don't know how to get to Sillycon Valley.
Dorothy:	Well, do you know how far it is to Sillycon Valley?
Bob 2:	*(shrugs)* Nope.
Dorothy:	Do you know if we'll find the Wicked Witch of the Web in Sillycon Valley?
Bob 2:	Can't say. *(turns away with nose in the air;* **Witch** *cackles and nods)*
Dorothy:	How can you work at an information station when you don't know anything?
Bob 2:	I don't know, *and*—I don't care.
Dorothy:	Do you even know your own name?
Bob 2:	Of course I do. It's Bob.
Dorothy:	*(looking quizzical)* Well … *Bob,* my name is Dorothy. I don't know how I ended up in Blahs, but I do know that I want to get back home to Nome ASAP. Would you care to help me?
Bob 2:	Not really … although I think there was a time when I might have cared about some things.
Bob 1:	What things?
Bob 2:	*(thinking)* I kind of remember caring about animals that were sick. *(excited)* Yes! That's it! I was going to be a veterinarian. I was enrolled in school, and I had my books and everything. Then, one day, I went on the Web to …
Bob 1:	And you got zapped. Right?
Witch:	*(cackles)* Heh, heh, heh! That's right! Zzzzzzap! And now Bob works for me, don't you, Bob?

Bob 2: Yeah, zapped. How did you know? The WWW zapped the care right out of me. Now you can show me a lost kitten or a bird with a broken wing, and I just turn away.

Dorothy: But didn't it feel good to care, Bob?

Bob 2: I don't remember. Seems like it should have, I guess. You know, I have this buzzing in my ears sometimes that reminds me of how my cat purred whenever I brushed its fur. *(thoughtfully)* I must have loved working with animals.

Dorothy: It sounds like you miss being a caring person, Bob. I think you'd better come with us to find the Wicked Witch of the Web. If she's the one who zapped you, maybe she can help you care again.

Witch: Did you say *help*? *Care*? Not a chance, little girl. Those words aren't even in my *wictionary*!

Bob 2: Maybe I will go with you. I don't care about this information station anyway. *(limps out from behind the table, barefooted)* Ooo! Ow!

Dorothy: What's wrong?

Bob 2: It's all these blisters and bruises and bumps on my feet from walking barefoot to work every day. *(limps around)* Ooo! Ow! Ouch!

Dorothy: Blisters and bruises and bumps? Oh my! I don't have any shoes in my tote bag, Bob, but I think I have something else that will help you. *(reaches into her tote and pulls out colorful socks)* Here! Put on these socks.

Witch: *(screeching)* No, Bob! Stop! Don't touch those … *(groans)* No. No! The colors! The colors!

Bob 2: *(putting on the socks)* Gee, thanks, Dorothy. I like the look—and my feet feel great!

Witch: Curses! Bob's not so blah anymore!

▶ *Dorothy steps between* **Bob 1** *and* **Bob 2**. *The three link arms and walk downstage.*

Narrator 1: So Dorothy set out again for Sillycon Valley …

Narrator 2: … but this time, with a Bob on each arm.

Bob 3: *(enters downstage left and blocks the road at center stage)* Who goes there? No one ever follows this road.

Dorothy: I'm Dorothy.

Bob 1: I'm Bob.

Bob 2: I'm Bob, too.

Dorothy: What's your name?

Bob 3: Bob.

Dorothy: Of course it is. I should have guessed. Well, Bob, we're looking for Sillycon Valley. Do you know if we're heading the right way?

Bob 3: You're heading the right way if you're looking for trouble.

Dorothy: Actually, we're looking for the WWW.

Bob 3: Then you're *really* looking for trouble. Don't you know what the WWW can do to you?

Bob 1: There's not much more she can do to me. She already zapped my energy.

Bob 2: And she zapped my caring about anything.

Bob 3: Well, that sounds familiar.

Dorothy: Oh? Did she do something to you, too?

Bob 3: Are you kidding? Uh, hello … look at me.
I haven't always been so drab and dull, you know.
I used to be an actor. I was creative. I had personality.
I had pizzazz.

Bob 1: Then, one day, you were on the Web …

Bob 2: … and you got zapped.

Bob 3: *(looking quizzically at Bob 1 and Bob 2)* Exactly. How did you know?

Bob 1: Been there.

Bob 2: Done that.

Bob 3: Just like that *(snaps fingers)*, my creativity was gone, and I've been a dud ever since. I still carry makeup and wigs around with me in this bag *(shows bag)*, but I never use them. I'm not even sure I remember what to do with them.

Dorothy: Sounds as if you need to face up to the WWW, Bob.

Bob 1: Yeah, like us. I want my energy back.

Bob 2: I want to care about things again.

Dorothy: And I want to get back home to Nome.

Bob 3: *(looking down at himself)* I can't face anybody or anything looking like this.

Witch: *(grinning wickedly)* Ah … That's my blah Bob.

Dorothy: I have something that might help, Bob. *(reaches into her tote, pulls out a colorful scarf, and hands it to Bob 3)* Here, put this on.

▶ **Bob 3** *wraps the scarf around his neck. Then he clears his throat and strikes a pose.*

Witch: What? *(stands up quickly)* Again with the colors? Curses! Not you too, Bob. Look at yourself! You're not blah anymore! *(plops down on her chair and sits slumped over, shaking her head)* Oh, what a world—what a world!

Bob 3: *(dramatically)* To be or not to be …

Dorothy: Wow! That's Shakespeare! It sounds as if you're making a comeback, Bob.

Bob 3: I hope you're right, Dorothy. So what are we waiting for? Let's go face the WWW. I want my creativity back!

▶ **Bobs** *get together to set off down the road.* **Dorothy** *stands still, looking a little dazed.*

Witch: Oh, you do, do you? Well, when I get through with you, Bob, you'll wish you were blah again! And as for you, my pretty, no one messes with the WWW and gets away with it. I'll get you—and your little tote, too!

▶ **Witch** *picks up her wand and skulks around looking for a hiding place where she can wait to ambush Dorothy and the Bobs.*

Bob 3: Is something wrong, Dorothy? All of a sudden, you look like *you've* been zapped.

Dorothy: Huh? Oh! No, Bob. It's nothing like that. I, uh … It's just, um … now that we're getting close to Sillycon Valley, I'm not feeling so brave anymore.

Bob 1: *(steps forward proudly)* Well, I am, Dorothy. I'll get you to the WWW PDQ! *(points arrow and faces stage right; motions energetically to the others)* Follow me, everyone!

▶ **Bob 2** and **Bob 3** *immediately line up behind* **Bob 1**. **Dorothy** *hesitates.*
Bob 2 *turns to her and holds out his hand.*

Bob 2:   Don't worry, Dorothy. I'll take care of you.

▶ **Dorothy** *gets in line behind* **Bob 2**. *All march (circling center stage, then heading stage left) with* **Bob 3** *lagging behind.*

Narrator 1:   Brave Bob led the way briskly. The others could hardly keep up. The other Bob watched for potholes to make sure that Dorothy didn't stumble.

Narrator 2:   Wait a minute. Wasn't there a third Bob? *(pause)* Oh, here he comes!

Bob 3:   *(dramatically)* There once was a lady from Mars …

Bob 1:   Come on, everyone. Keep moving. We're almost there.

Bob 3:   *(dramatically)* … whose eyeballs looked rather like stars.

▶ **Witch** *swoops in downstage left and waves her wand in front of Bob 1.*
All stop abruptly and cluster together.

Witch: Where do you think you're going? And why have you Bobs left your posts? *(brandishing her wand and addressing each Bob, in turn, starting with Bob 3)* Take off that ridiculous scarf, Bob! And you, Bob, go to your information station—immediately! As for you, Bob, take your arrow and …

Bob 1:   *(stepping forward and speaking bravely)* The only thing I'm going to do with this arrow is use it to help Dorothy find her way home.

Bob 2:   And I'm going to make sure she gets there safely.

Bob 3:   *(peering at the witch as he approaches her)* I hope you don't mind my saying this, Your Wickedness, but you look awful!

Witch: *(shaking her wand at Bob 3)* What did you just say to me?

Bob 3:   I said, "You look awful!" Come on … What's with the green makeup? And that wart is just plain *ugly*. Your hairstyle isn't right for your face, and your outfit doesn't do a thing for your figure.

Witch: *(suddenly downcast and sniveling)* Now why'd you have to go and say things like that? Running everything around here hasn't been easy, you know. I never have any time for myself anymore. I used to look good! Some people even said I glowed. *(brief pause)* And I was nice, too! Why, I used to …

Bob 3:   Stop whining and turn toward me. I want to get a good look at you. *(**Witch** faces Bob 3)* You really have some good features. Just look at those cheekbones. I don't like to brag, but I could have you glowing again in no time.

Witch: You could?

Bob 3:   Yes, indeed! Gather 'round, everyone. I might need a little assistance.

▶ *Dorothy* and the *Bobs* surround the witch, hiding her from the audience's view. *Bob 3* and *Dorothy* pull items out of their bags and mime appropriate movements, ultimately switching the witch's mask from the Wicked Witch to the Wonderful Witch.

Bob 3:   First, let's change that green tint you're wearing to something more natural. *(pause)* Ah! Much better. Now about that wart. I'll use some of this and a little of that. Yes, that works. Can't even see that pesky bump anymore.

Bob 1:   Can you do anything with her hair?

Dorothy: We can curl it! *(hands a curling iron to Bob 3)* And I think I have some earrings in here somewhere. *(rummages through her tote)* Here they are! Hey! Look what else I found—a tiara! I forgot I had this. It will look great on you! *(hands tiara to Bob 3)*

Bob 3:	Oh dear. The outfit. All this black is so yesterday. But wait! I have just the thing! *(drapes his colorful scarf around the witch's shoulders and then **all** step back so the witch can be seen by the audience)* Voila! What do you think, everyone?
Narrator 1:	Bob and the other Bob *oohed* and *ahhed*.
Narrator 2:	Bob and Dorothy beamed with pride at their creation.
Dorothy:	*(pulling a hand mirror out of her tote and holding it up in front of the witch)* You look stunning! Here. See for yourself.
Witch:	*(pleased but somewhat subdued)* Is that me? Oh my.
Bob 2:	*(caringly)* You feel a lot better now, don't you?
Witch:	*(brightening)* I do feel better, Bob. But … *(looking around sadly)* now Blahs looks so gloomy.
Bob 3:	Then let's make some changes in Blahs, too! All it needs is a little creativity and color.
Bob 1:	First, let's get rid of this black asphalt road. I could put in a sturdy brick one. And it could be red or blue or purple … any color of the rainbow.
Witch:	My favorite color used to be yellow.
Bob 1:	Yellow it is, then! I'll build you a yellow brick road.
Bob 2:	Wait a minute, everybody! What about Dorothy? Nothing in Blahs would have changed if Dorothy hadn't come along. Now we need to help her get back home to Nome.
Witch:	Oh, that's easy!

▶ *Witch walks to center stage and waves her wand.*
Rainbow 1 and Rainbow 2 enter upstage right and move quickly to center stage.

Witch: *(stepping back to reveal the rainbow)* Just walk under the rainbow, Dorothy, and you'll be home before you can blink.

Dorothy: Oh, thank you! Why, you're not wicked at all. You're *wonderful*! *(hugs the witch and waves to the Bobs)* Goodbye, Bobs!

Narrator 1: As Dorothy walked toward the rainbow, Bob, Bob, Bob, and the WWW went back to their plans for transforming Blahs.

Narrator 2: They even decided to change the name from *Blahs* to *Ahs*!

► *Witch* and *Bobs* move downstage left and stop at the exit to look back at Dorothy. *Dorothy* has stopped under rainbow to look back at them.

Bob 2: *(to the other Bobs)* Do you think she'll be okay?

► *All* wave to each other. *Witch* and *Bobs* exit downstage left. *Dorothy* walks under the rainbow and sits down on the floor *(looking dazed)*, stage left of the arcade props. *Rainbow* exits downstage right. *Tracy* enters upstage right and turns "Information" sign to "Arcade." *Ty* and *Tory* enter upstage left with joysticks. *All* resume their earlier "freeze" positions and then rush over to Dorothy. *(Tracy* kneels next to her; *Ty* and *Tory* stand near her, looking on with concern.)*

Tracy: Do you think she'll be okay?

Tory: Look! She blinked!

Dorothy: Where am I?

Ty: You're in Nome, silly … at the arcade.

Dorothy: Oh, thank goodness! *(Tory, Tracy, and Ty help Dorothy to her feet.)* I thought I'd never get back.

Tracy: Back? Back from where?

Dorothy: Uh … no place! I just meant that I'm glad to see you guys. And take my word for it … *(looks around and smiles)* there's no place like Nome!

► *All* exit upstage right, chatting and laughing.

How to Make the Masks and Props

The following pages contain full-color, easy-to-assemble masks and props for all of the plays in *How to Do Plays from Favorite Tales*. Color-coded pages make the materials for each play easy to locate, and the name of the character or prop is printed on the back of each item for easy identification.

Play	Color Code	Pages
Things Could Always Be Worse	Blue	102–115
The Magic Pasta Pot	Orange	117–127
What Is an Elephant?	Green	129–143
The King Who Would Not Laugh	Purple	145–161
Dorothy in the Land of Blahs	Red	163–175

Assembling a Mask

You will need:
- laminating film
- scissors
- craft knife
- string or yarn

Directions:

1. Laminate the page with the mask and cut out the mask along the dashed lines. *(Laminating is strongly suggested for added durability and to keep the mask looking like new.)* ✳

2. Use a craft knife to cut along the dashed lines around the bottom and sides of the eyes. Do not cut through the solid part of the line at the top of the eye. Fold each eye up slightly along the solid line to form slits for the mask wearer to see through. *(You may also choose to cut all the way around the eyes to make eyeholes.)*

3. Poke a small hole through the tiny white dot on each side of the mask and thread string or yarn through each hole. Knot the string or yarn securely in place at the front of the mask.

   ✳ For best results, masks that are not laminated should be reinforced with construction paper. *(See steps 3 and 4 on page 12.)*

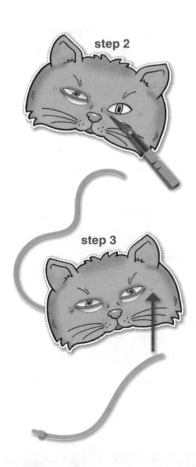

step 2

step 3

Things Could Always Be Worse

How to Make the Chicken Prop

How to assemble the prop

1. Laminate, if possible, the chicken *(page 103)* and the basket *(page 105)*.

2. Cut out both figures along the dashed lines.

3. Cut along the dashed line in the basket to open a long slit for the chicken to rest in.

4. Tuck the bottom of the chicken into the slit and tape the back of the chicken to the back of the basket to hold the two pieces together securely.

How to make the prop stand up

Use a Bookend

Lean the prop against a metal bookend. Use a bookend that's small enough to fit behind the prop without being seen.

back view

Use Clay

Shape a lump of clay so that it rests flat on a table. Cut a slit across the top of the lump and position the prop in the slit. Press the clay against the front and back of the prop to keep the prop standing up straight.

front view

Make a Paper Stand

1. Cut a strip of flexible cardboard that is 10 inches (25 cm) long and 5 inches (13 cm) high.

2. Fold the cardboard strip in half.

3. Fold back 2 inches (5 cm) at each end to make an accordion fold. The strip will look like the letter T.

4. Tape the two ends of the strip to the back of the prop, with the folded middle section sticking out.

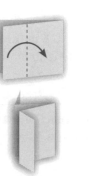

back view

Things Could Always Be Worse

© Evan-Moor Corp. • EMC 3332 • How to Do Plays from Favorite Tales

Things Could Always Be Worse

Chicken

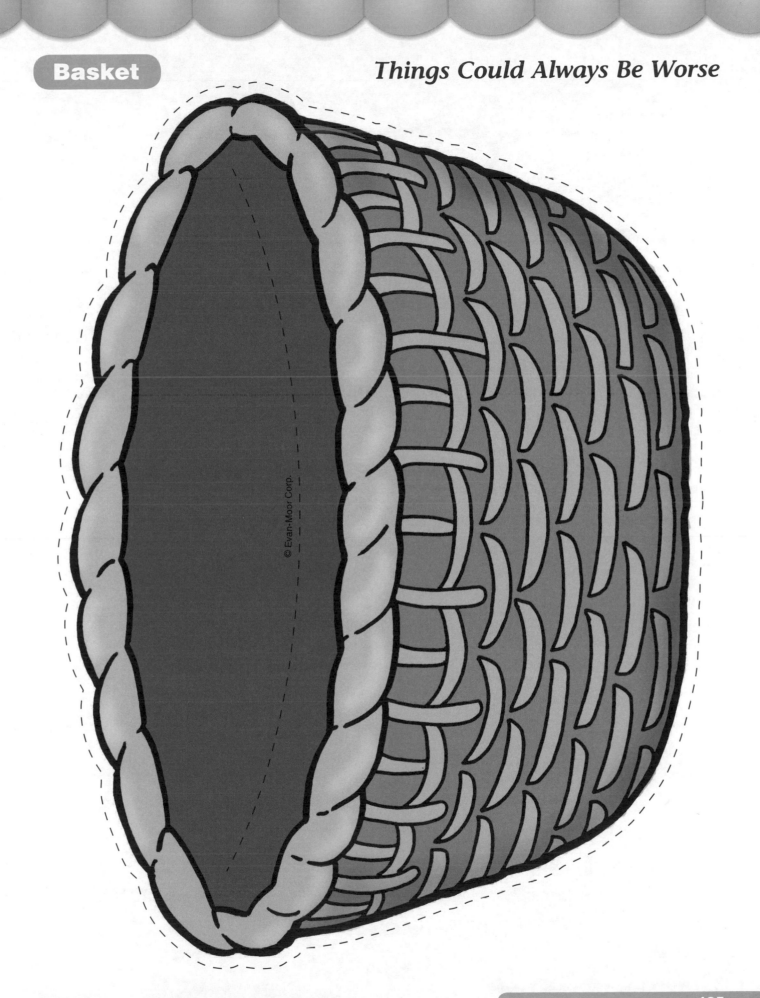

© Evan-Moor Corp.

Things Could Always Be Worse

Basket

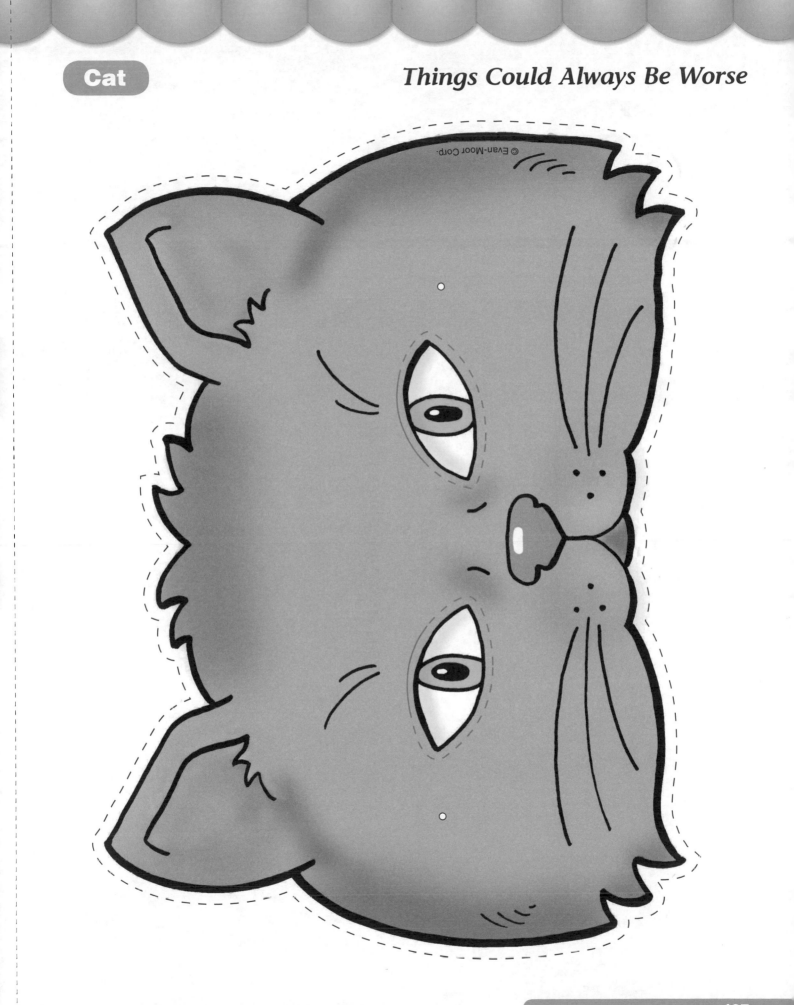

Things Could Always Be Worse

Cat

Things Could Always Be Worse

Dog

Things Could Always Be Worse

Rooster

Things Could Always Be Worse

Cow

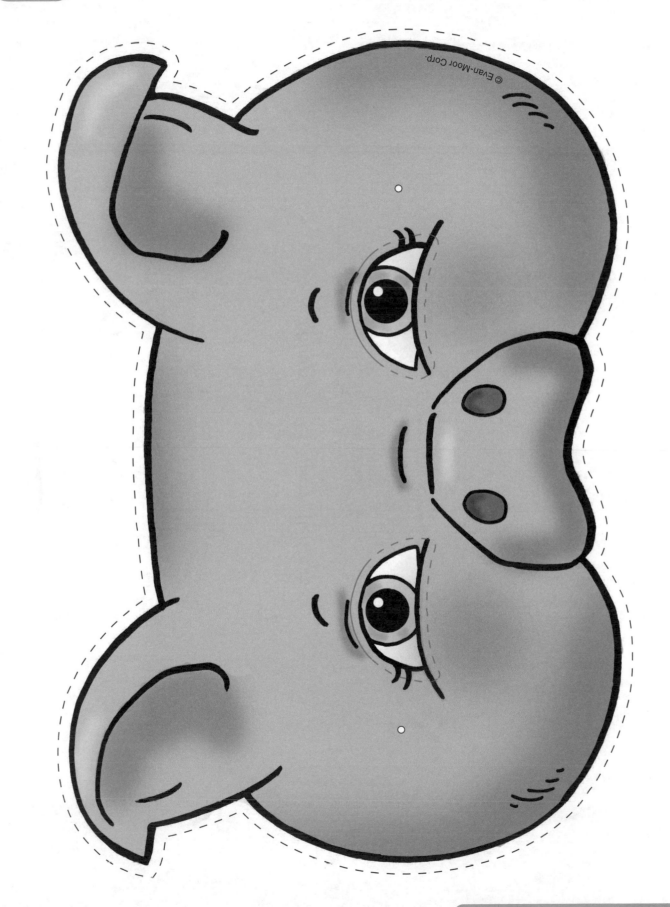

Things Could Always Be Worse

Pig

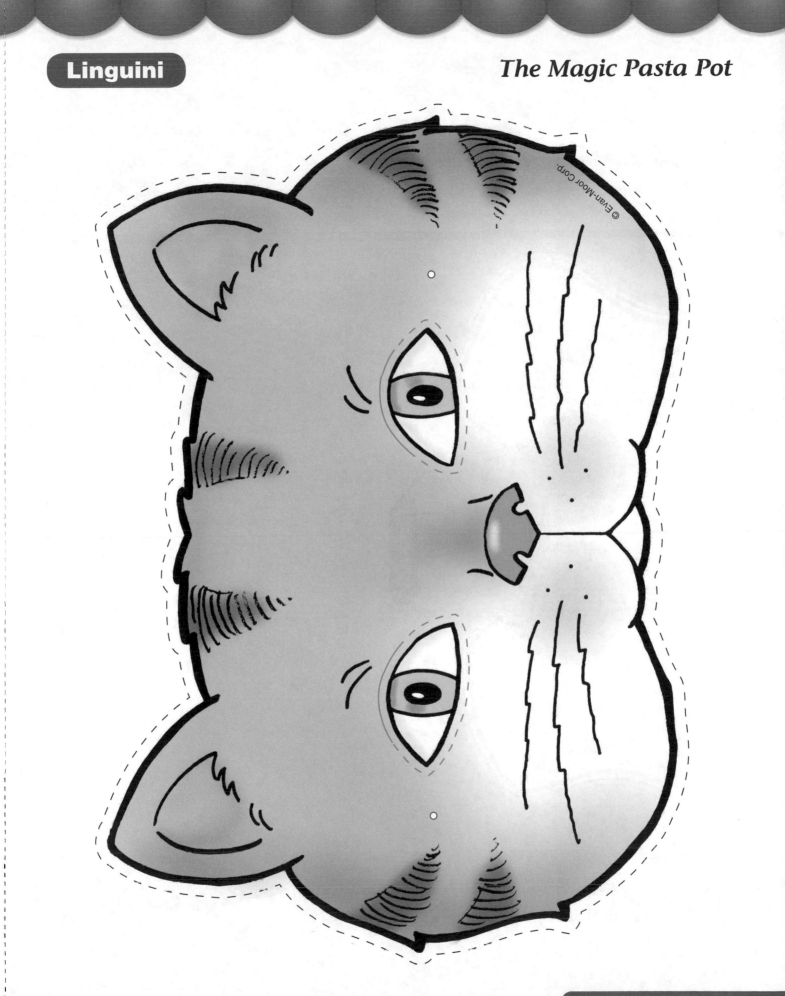

The Magic Pasta Pot

Linguini

Pasta Pot *(top left)*

See page 30 for assembly instructions.

The Magic Pasta Pot

Pasta Pot (top left)

© Evan-Moor Corp.

See page 30 for assembly instructions.

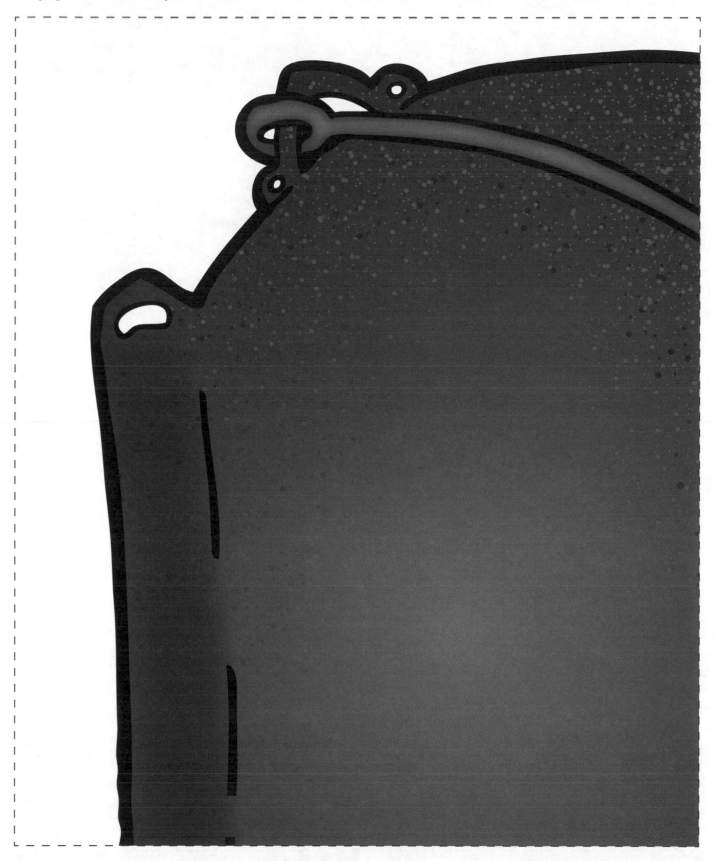

The Magic Pasta Pot

Pasta Pot *(top right)*

© Evan-Moor Corp.

See page 30 for assembly instructions.

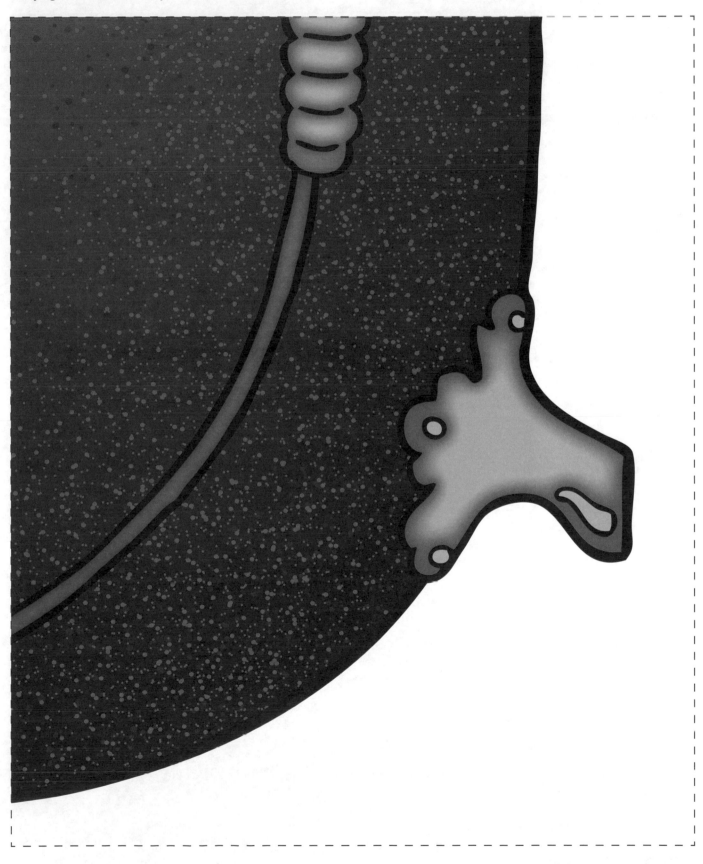

The Magic Pasta Pot

Pasta Pot (bottom left)

© Evan-Moor Corp.

Pasta Pot *(bottom right)*

See page 30 for assembly instructions.

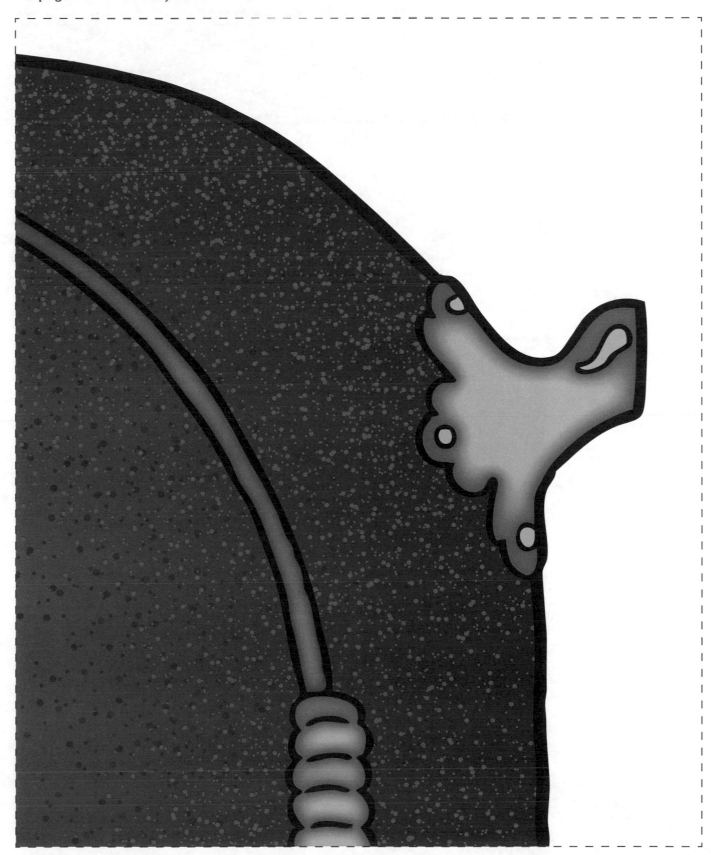

The Magic Pasta Pot

Pasta Pot (bottom right)

© Evan-Moor Corp.

See page 30 for assembly instructions.

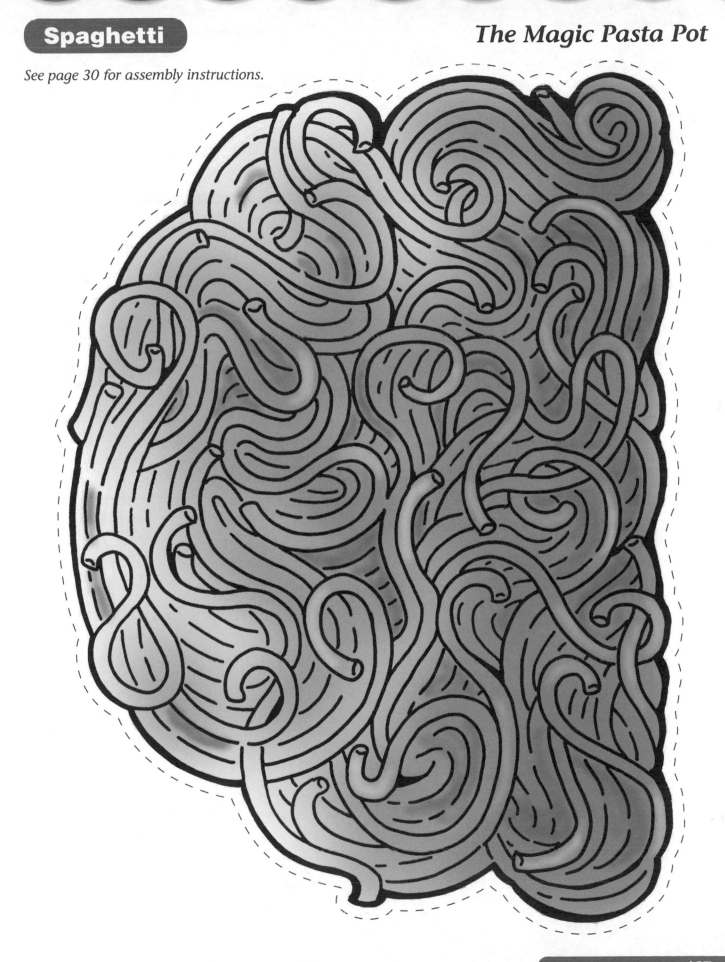

The Magic Pasta Pot

Spaghetti

See page 49 for assembly instructions.

What Is an Elephant?

Elephant *(top #1)*

© Evan-Moor Corp.

See page 49 for assembly instructions.

What Is an Elephant?

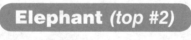

Elephant *(top #2)*

See page 49 for assembly instructions.

What Is an Elephant?

Elephant *(top #3)*

See page 49 for assembly instructions.

What Is an Elephant?

Elephant *(top #4)*

Elephant *(bottom #1)*

See page 49 for assembly instructions.

What Is an Elephant?

Elephant *(bottom #1)*

© Evan-Moor Corp.

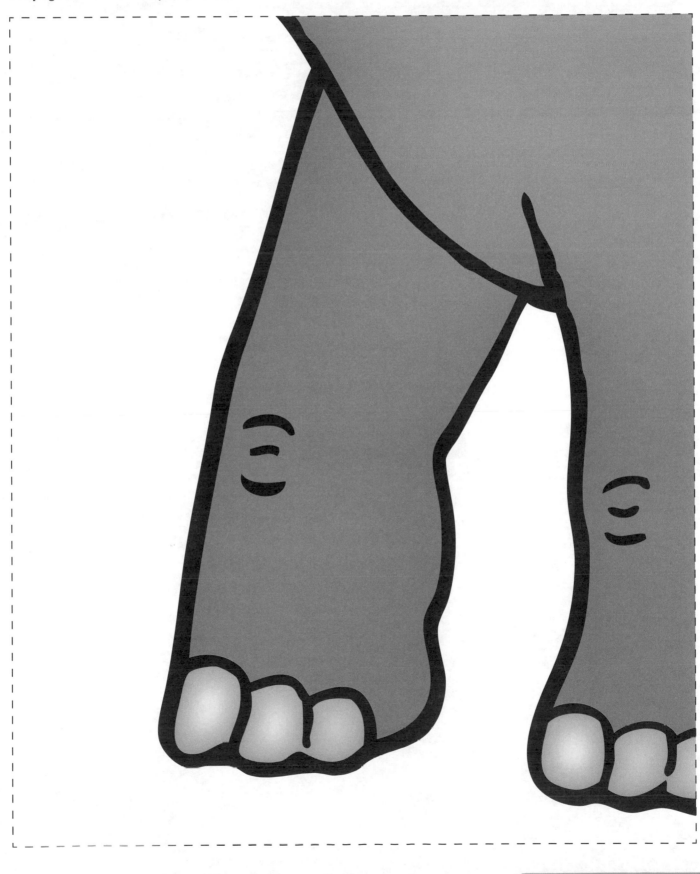

What Is an Elephant?

Elephant *(bottom #2)*

© Evan-Moor Corp.

See page 49 for assembly instructions.

What Is an Elephant?

Elephant *(bottom #3)*

See page 49 for assembly instructions.

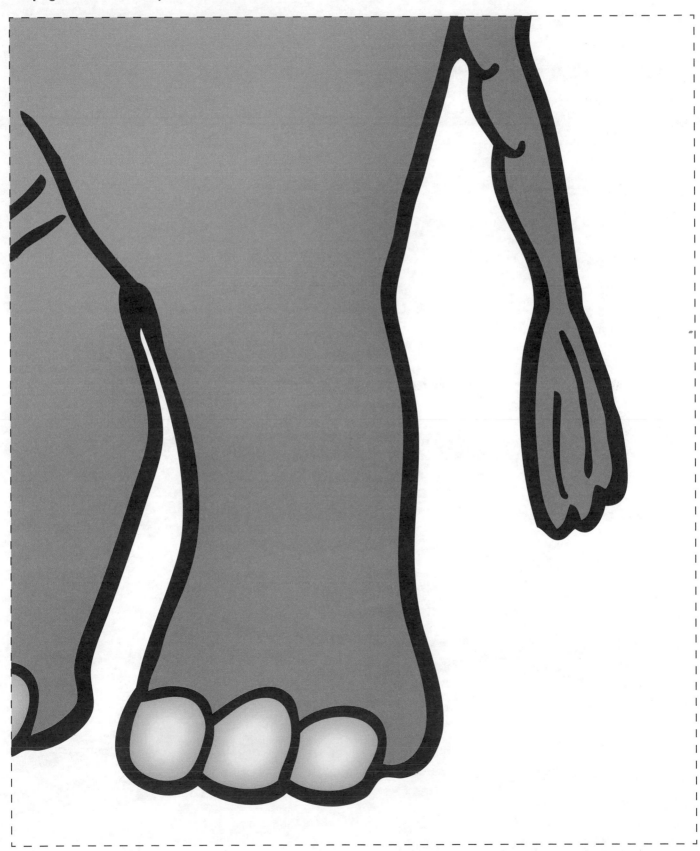

What Is an Elephant?

Elephant *(bottom #4)*

How to Do Plays from Favorite Tales • EMC 3332 • © Evan-Moor Corp.

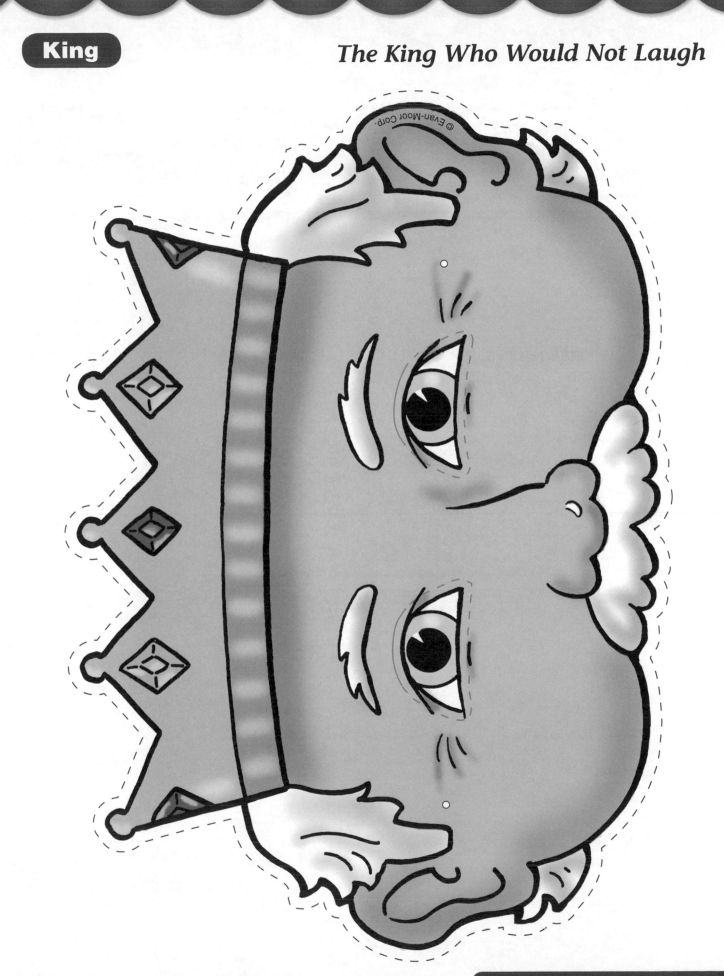

The King Who Would Not Laugh

King

The King Who Would Not Laugh

See page 66 for assembly instructions.

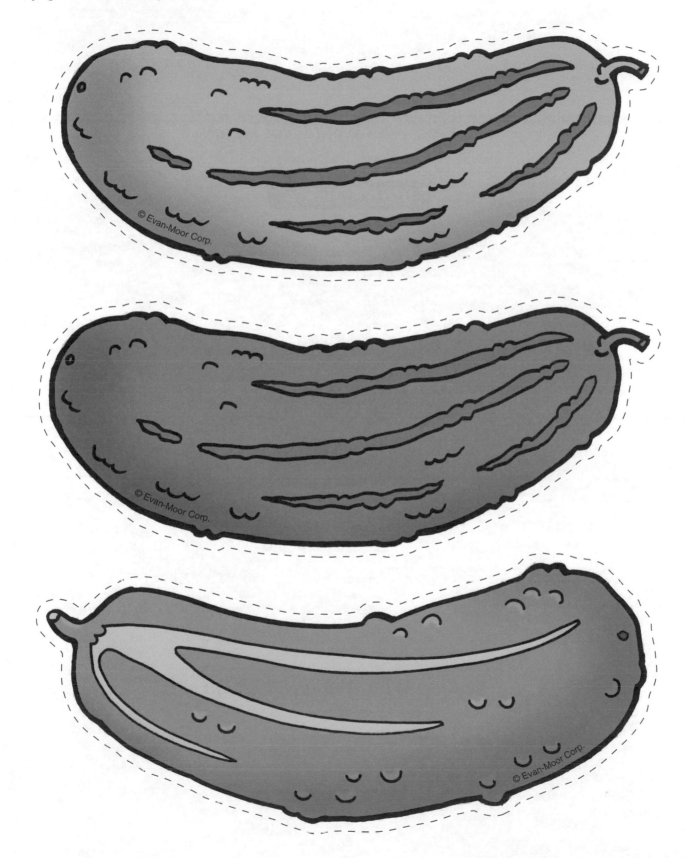

© Evan-Moor Corp.

© Evan-Moor Corp.

© Evan-Moor Corp.

The King Who Would Not Laugh

The King Who Would Not Laugh

The King Who Would Not Laugh

Bozo's Pickle

Boo-boo's Flower

The King Who Would Not Laugh

Follow the directions for the Jokester's Badge. (See page 153.)

© Evan-Moor Corp.

The King Who Would Not Laugh

Boo-boo's Flower

Directions:

1. Cut out the bow tie along the dashed lines and laminate it, if possible, for added durability. If the bow tie is not laminated, use it as a template to trace the shape onto flexible cardboard or heavy construction paper. Cut out the shape and glue it onto the back of the bow tie. (For best results, use a glue stick or rubber cement.)

2. Poke small holes on each side of the bow tie's center section and thread string or yarn through each hole. Knot the string or yarn securely in place at the front of the bow tie. (Make sure that the string or yarn is long enough to be tied comfortably around the student's neck.)

© Evan-Moor Corp.

The King Who Would Not Laugh

Bobo's Bow Tie

Jokester's Badge

The King Who Would Not Laugh

Directions:

1 Cut out the badge along the dashed lines and laminate it, if possible.

2 Tape a large safety pin on the back of the badge, about halfway above the center point.

3 Pin the badge to the student's clothing.

back view

The King Who Would Not Laugh

Jokester's Badge

© Evan-Moor Corp.

The King Who Would Not Laugh

Jokester's Badge

© Evan-Moor Corp.

© Evan-Moor Corp.

The King Who Would Not Laugh

Jokester's Badge

The King Who Would Not Laugh

Jokester's Badge

The King Who Would Not Laugh

Goofy

The King Who Would Not Laugh

Follow steps 1 and 2 in the directions for The Fool's Scepter. (See page 66.)

The King Who Would Not Laugh

See page 66 for assembly instructions.

The King Who Would Not Laugh

Fool's Scepter

Dorothy in the Land of Blahs

Wicked Witch

Dorothy in the Land of Blahs

Wonderful Witch

Witch's Wand (top)

Directions:

1 Cut out the top and bottom sections of the lightning bolt *(pages 167 and 169)* along the dashed lines and laminate each section, if possible.

2 Lay both sections flat on a table with the front sides down and the straight ends together. Apply clear tape along the seam to hold the sections together.

3 If the sections are not laminated, cut a strip of very stiff cardboard, 1 inch (2.5 cm) wide by 10 inches (25 cm) long, and lay it across the seam. Tape down the cardboard securely to reinforce the seam.

4 Tape a ruler or a paint stirring stick onto the back of the lightning bolt, at the bottom, leaving at least 7 inches (18 cm) to use as a handle.

back view

front view

Dorothy in the Land of Blahs

Witch's Wand *(top)*

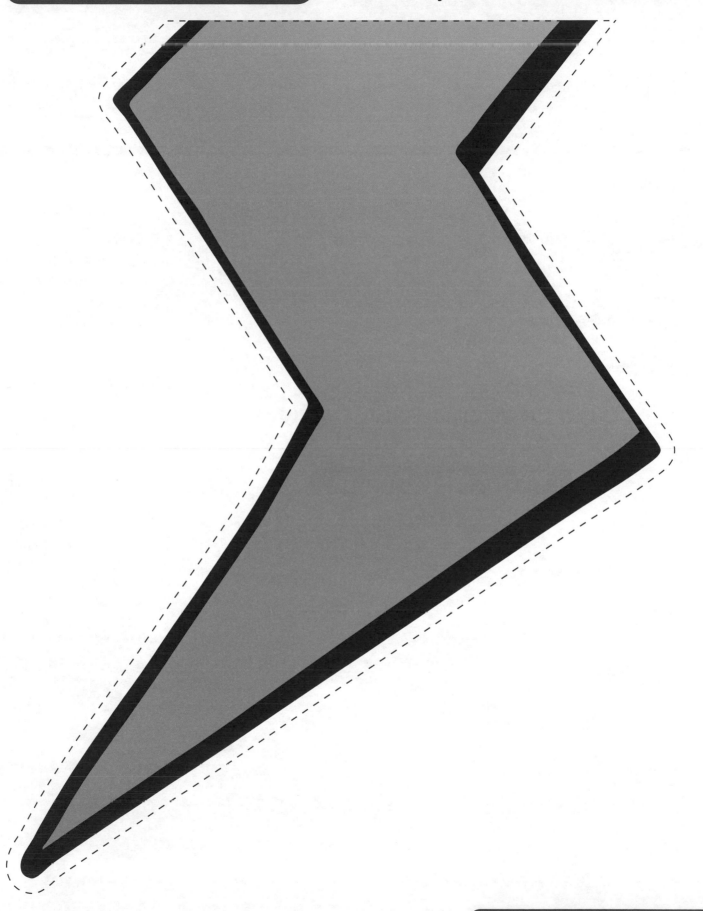

Dorothy in the Land of Blahs

Witch's Wand *(bottom)*

© Evan-Moor Corp.

Directions:

1 Cut out the three sections of the rainbow *(pages 171, 173, and 175)* along the dashed lines and laminate each section, if possible.

If the sections are not laminated, use them as templates to trace around each shape on very stiff cardboard. Cut out the cardboard shapes and glue them onto the backs of the rainbow sections. (For best results, use a glue stick or rubber cement.)

back view

2 Lay all three sections flat on a table with the colored sides down, arranging them to form an arc. Apply clear tape along the seams between the sections to hold them together.

3 Tape the top 2 inches (5 cm) of a large craft stick securely to the back of the rainbow at each end to make handles for holding up the prop.

front view

Dorothy in the Land of Blahs

Rainbow *(left)*

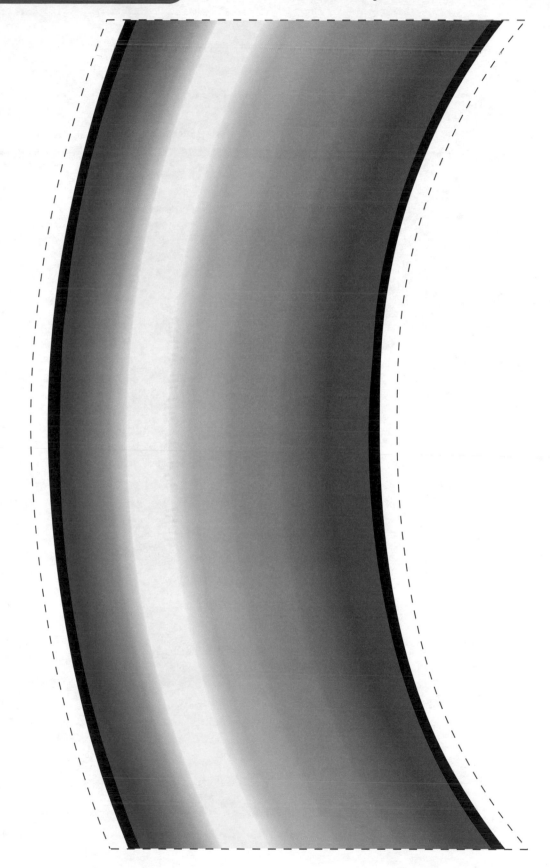

Dorothy in the Land of Blahs

Rainbow *(middle)*

© Evan-Moor Corp.

Dorothy in the Land of Blahs

Rainbow *(right)*